The Legacy Continues ...

Stories of Precious Blood Sisters
Continuing the Legacy
of
Mother Maria Anna Brunner

CPPS Biographies Project
Volume IV

Sisters of the Precious Blood
Dayton, Ohio

WovenWord Press

The Legacy Continues . . .
Sisters of the Precious Blood
WovenWord Press
811 Mapleton Avenue
Boulder, Colorado
80304
Copyright © 2003

ISBN 0 9719383-3-4

Dedication

To the many Sisters of the Precious Blood
whose lives of humble, unselfish service
were largely unheralded,
but who faithfully lived the tradition
of work and prayer

We dedicate this book also to
Sister Cordelia Gast
who was a member of the CPPS Biography Project team
until her death on May 15, 2002.
Her presence, knowledge, support, and inspiration
were sorely missed
in the production of this volume.

Acknowledgments

Special thanks to:

❖ Sister Maryann Bremke, President of the Congregation, for her generous support and enthusiastic encouragement;

❖ Sister Noreen Jutte, Congregational Archivist, and her assistant, Linda Hageman, for providing necessary documentation and photos;

❖ Sisters Eleanor McNally, Eileen Monnin, Canice Werner, and Patricia Crother, CSJ for their careful reading of the manuscript;

❖ All who have affirmed, supported and encouraged us to continue this project;

❖ Sheila Durkin Dierks and Vicki McVey of WovenWord Press for their help and encouragement.

CPPS Biographies Project
Volume IV

Project Director	Helen Weber CPPS
Writers	Rose Margaret Broerman CPPS
	Eleanor McNally CPPS
	Helen Weber CPPS
Editor	Anne Agnew CPPS
Researcher	Canice Werner CPPS

Volume IV is the final volume of the *Legacy Series,* at least for the present time. Unfortunately, we do not have at hand sufficient written records to develop additional biographies of non-contemporary sisters.

Through remembering and storytelling, we continue to live the legacy of Maria Anna Brunner. We are grateful to all who have contributed to the production of the *Legacy Series.* We hope that these slim volumes have enriched the self-understanding of members of the Congregation.

The *Heritage Series,* initiated in 2002 with Volume I, *The Work of Their Hands,* will contain additional information about the Sisters of the Precious Blood and their ministries.

As in previous volumes, we have not used the title "Sister" after the initial introduction, except in the case of Major Superiors. A few minor adjustments in grammar and spelling have been made in quotations for the sake of clarity. Italics are used when the subject of the story is quoted directly.

Contents

Volume IV

Preface

Then the Lord answered and said:
Write down the vision clearly upon the tablets,
so that one can read it readily.
For the vision still has its time, presses on to fulfillment,
and will not disappoint. . . .
Habakkuk 2: 2-3

Although Maria Anna Brunner did not write down her vision for her followers, her legacy, nevertheless, has been lived out over the years in the lives of her daughters, the Sisters of the Precious Blood. By reading and reflecting on the stories of the sisters who preceded them, women dedicated to the Precious Blood of Jesus today may re-discover the vision, the challenge and the hope inspired by their foundress.

This, the final volume of the *Legacy Series,* opens with stories of four sisters, each of whom is well-known, perhaps even legendary, in the history of the Congregation.

Following these stories, "Healing Hands" presents tales of sisters who spent their religious lives generously serving others in the health care ministry. Through the accounts of these sisters who are representative of many others, a brief sketch of the Congregation's involvement in health care emerges.

The last section of this volume, "Lives of Humble Service," focuses on the many sisters who were involved in work commonly referred to as General or Domestic Arts. Their lives, perhaps, most closely resemble that of Mother Brunner and the earliest sisters. These sisters performed the essential tasks of cleaning, cooking, sewing, washing—the humble chores often too little valued. Their daily work, made holy through hours of prayer before the Blessed Sacrament, exemplified the Benedictine tradition of prayer and work adopted by the Congregation.

In this volume, as in the previous books in this series, the stories of the sisters' lives illustrate the continuing fulfillment of Mother Brunner's vision. Through these written words, may her vision be read and remembered.

Uniquely Gifted

Stories of four singularly talented women
whose generous response to Community needs
earned for them near legendary status
in the history of the Congregation

**By Helen Weber CPPS, Eleanor McNally CPPS,
and Rose Margaret Broerman CPPS**

Sister Mary Grace Pratt (1878-1979)

By Helen Weber

On a steamy summer day in Cincinnati, Ohio in 1928, a nun in traditional black garb, stepped purposefully through the debris of a dusty construction site. Obviously at home in this environment and apparently oblivious of the sweltering day, she entered the building still under construction on the corner of Fenwick and Quatman.

Noticing the nun approach with a roll of blueprints under her arm, the foreman on the job hurried to meet her. He showed an obvious respect for her, not only because she was a religious, but also because she understood the building profession. While listening carefully to her insistence that the school must be ready for occupancy for the new academic year, he looked around and slowly shook his head. Politely but firmly, she urged him to push his men even harder.

During the previous two months, Sister Grace Pratt, recently appointed principal of this new Regina High School, had been diligently planning for its opening. With a few other sisters who would teach in the school, she had spent the early part of the summer visiting parishes and recruiting students. Now it was time to prepare classrooms for the 250 girls enrolled. Thanks to the prayers of the sisters and the hard work of the construction crew, classes at the school began only a few weeks late.

Ground for the school had been broken in the previous fall, and the cornerstone laid in late April. The men had accomplished a herculean feat putting up, in so short a time, the four-story building, eventually to serve 500 students. Despite the fact that Grace, during the 1927-28 academic year, was at Catholic University in Washington DC working on her doctorate, she had been involved in designing and planning the building since its inception. Though trained to be a mathematics teacher, Grace was to have a great influence in the Community as an architect and designer.

What sort of woman, and a nun at that, could be so accepted and heeded in the male-dominated world of architecture and construction in the 1920s?

Background

Nestled in the rolling hills of central Ohio, about 40 miles northeast of Columbus is the pleasant little town of Mt. Vernon. Near state parks and lovely lakes with its picturesque beauty of surrounding peaceful hills and valleys and the winding course of the Kokosing River, Mt. Vernon is a mecca for modern-day campers, bikers and vacationers. Here amid this unspoiled beauty, John Franklin Pratt, Grace's father, was born in mid-19th century. John found his bride, Catherine Cecelia Konig, in Danville, another small Ohio town in Knox County.

Documents from colonial times in America include the name, Pratt. With the opening of Ohio to settlers in the early 1800s, the Pratt and the Konig families homesteaded Knox County. The town of Mt. Vernon, settled by pioneers from Virginia, Maryland, New Jersey and Pennsylvania, received its name from the home of President George Washington in Virginia.

Agnes Gertrude Pratt was born in Mt. Vernon on May 20, 1878. Records do not reveal much information about her siblings. Her brothers, Harry and Charles, both died in the 1940s. Her sister (name unknown), who married William Durbin, died in 1952. Agnes was to outlive them all by many years.

Entering the Congregation

During Agnes's childhood, her family moved to Ft. Recovery, Ohio. After attending high school there for two years, she entered the convent of the Sisters of the Precious Blood at Maria Stein, Ohio on June 21, 1893. The Congregation had founded an elementary school in Ft. Recovery in 1881, though there is no record that Agnes attended this school.

Mother Ludovica Scharf welcomed 15-year-old Agnes into the Community, and Sister Margaret Schlachter, mistress of novices, guided her through the early stages of religious formation. When she became a novice on September 5, 1894, Agnes received the name of Sister Mary Gratia.

The novitiate, including Normal School training, passed quickly for Gratia and her classmates. While still a novice, she began her long career in education by teaching in Minister, Ohio. She pronounced temporary vows on September 28, 1897. For the next several years, she continued studying in the Normal School while periodically taking on short teaching assignments, usually for one year, in St. Wendelin and Minister, Ohio and at Precious Blood School in Ft. Wayne, Indiana. From 1902 to 1911, Gratia gained valuable classroom experience teaching at Immaculate Conception School in Celina, Ohio. On August 11, 1905, having been in the Community for 12 years and now 27 years old, she made final vows as a member of the Congregation.

When Victoria Drees, director of the Normal School, was elected to the Community Council in 1911, the School was in need of another seasoned educator. Even though Gratia did not possess a degree at that time, superiors summoned her from Celina to instruct novices in the art of teaching. Shortly afterwards, Gratia and Sister Rosalie Alt were assigned to study at the Catholic University of America in Washington DC. There in 1916, they received their bachelor's degrees, the first two members of the Congregation to do so.

Superiors soon realized that a bachelor's degree was insufficient for an instructor in a teacher-training institution. Also, in order to obtain a license for the Normal School and to abide by state regulations, its teachers had to have higher education credentials. Consequently, both Rosalia and Gratia returned to Washington, one at a time, to obtain master's degrees. Rosalia studied during the academic year, 1916-17, while Gratia taught in the Normal School. The next year they switched places.

St. Mary 's, Dayton

At some point during these years of study at Catholic University, Gratia changed her name to the English version, Grace. After receiving her MA degree in 1918, Grace went to St. Mary's Parish in Dayton where she was both principal of the school and superior of the sisters living and working there. During her years at the school, she established a reputation as an outstanding educator.

Sister Mary Grace Pratt

As demonstrated in later life, Grace had a great interest in and an obvious aptitude for architecture and artistic design. Sister Florentine Gregory, who was a child at St. Mary's during the time of Grace's principalship, provides the first record of her ventures into these fields:

> I knew Sister Grace Pratt as the principal of St. Mary's School in Dayton. She came when I was in the lower grades to replace a much loved Sister Mary Genevieve Koselke. As a child I was rather afraid of her, but during my high school years, that abated some. I well remember sitting in St. Mary's Church one Sunday when the sanctuary was being renovated and hearing Father (not yet Monsignor) Bernard Beckmeyer say that Sister Grace had drawn the plan for the marble flooring and each piece had fit perfectly.

According to the custom of the times, St. Mary's Parish had a three-year commercial high school to provide business training for young women after grade school. The

Community had similar schools in Wapakoneta and Celina, Ohio. While principal at St. Mary's, Grace expanded the commercial high school to a four-year, co-educational full-curriculum school. It received accreditation in 1921, but remained in existence only until 1928 when, due to archdiocesan planning, the Sisters of Notre Dame opened Julienne High School and the Brothers of Mary initiated Chaminade.

Before the closure of the high school, however, Grace had left St. Mary's to return to teaching in the Normal School at Salem Heights. During 1926-27, while teaching there, she became involved in another architectural project. In 1921, Mother Emma Nunlist had been approached by a group of Catholic women in Dayton requesting that the Congregation consider building and staffing a home for the aging. Because construction of the motherhouse in Dayton was then underway, the new project was postponed until the completion of Salem Heights in 1923.

After Mother Agreda Sperber's election in 1924, the Congregation began to consider the proposal for a home for the aging. In 1926 superiors decided to build the facility on motherhouse grounds. To Grace's delight, the Congregation asked her to work with the architects in planning this building. Its unique design, with five wings extending from a center rotunda thereby assuring maximum daylight and cross ventilation, made it strikingly different from other such institutions. Grace's influence in combining beauty and function was evident. Because the superiors had other plans for her, however, she could not remain in Dayton to oversee the completion of the Maria Joseph Home, as the facility was named. Grace was sent back to Catholic University in 1927 to work towards a doctorate degree necessary for the Community's teacher training program. The Maria Joseph Home for the Aged opened for occupancy on September 1, 1930 when only two of the projected five wings were completed.

Regina High School

With the growth of population in urban areas came an increased demand for high schools. State laws and new

7

expectations in curriculum called for expensive and sophisti-
cated educational facilities beyond those which most parishes
could afford. The Sisters of the Precious Blood and other religious communities became involved in the movement to
build archdiocesan high schools. *Not With Silver or Gold*, the
history of the Sisters of the Precious Blood, gives an account of
this time:

> Before his death [in 1925] Archbishop [Henry]
> Mueller had inaugurated a plan for meeting the
> needs of Catholic secondary education in the diocese.
> The practice of having small high schools maintained
> by individual parishes was to give way in cities to the
> central high school system. Modern high schools
> were to be erected and equipped by the diocese or by
> various teaching Orders at their own expense, and
> each school was to be supported by assessments on
> the parishes. . . . Thus educational facilities offered to
> Catholic youth would compare favorably with those
> of the best public institutions and would be an incen-
> tive for parents to keep their growing boys and girls
> under Catholic influence (p. 355).

Archbishop Mueller died before the plan could be carried
out, but his successor, John T. McNicholas, also a strong advo-
cate of Catholic education, moved quickly to implement it.
Mother Agreda received word that the Congregation was
expected to erect and staff a high school in Cincinnati to serve
parishes in the northwest section, including Norwood. It
seems harsh and almost unbelievable that the Archbishop
could order a Congregation to do this, but there is no evidence
that superiors did not quickly comply. Finding an appropriate
site for the school, however, presented a problem. Again,
quoting *Not With Silver or Gold:*

> Various locations for the building were contem-
> plated. . . . But the location upon which they [the
> superiors] had set their heart was a vacant lot belong-
> ing to the diocese, situated on the corner of Fenwick

Avenue and Quatman Street in Norwood, opposite Mount St. Mary Seminary. When Mother Agreda requested Archbishop McNicholas to sell her the property, he absolutely refused. She was not disturbed. With her usual equanimity she went home and asked the Sisters to pray that the Archbishop would relent. Prayer won the day. Without further solicitation on the part of the Sisters, Archbishop McNicholas finally offered to deed them the land. In the fall of 1927 the wooded area was cleared and ground broken for the proposed building (p. 356).

The Congregation's chief concern was the choice of a sister capable of leading this new venture. Although Grace was studying for her doctorate at Catholic University, superiors decided that she was the person with the needed qualities. She was directed to discontinue her studies at the close of the academic year and to take charge of the new high school. Unfortunately, she would never finish the work on the doctorate.

When Grace learned that she was to be the founding principal of Regina High School, the architect in her rose to the

Regina High School

challenge. One can imagine her, while still at Catholic University, drawing plans, perhaps doodling, during a lecture. She may have come home during the Christmas vacation to meet with the architects, or perhaps she kept in touch with them by phone or letter. It is hard to reconstruct the processes by which she became so influential in the building of Regina High School.

When Grace returned from Washington to Cincinnati in the summer of 1928, most of the actual construction of the high school was completed. As mentioned earlier, while she supervised the completion of the internal details of the structure, she was also busy recruiting students. Eventually, it all came together, and Regina High School opened its door on October 1, 1928. *Not With Silver or Gold* paints a vivid picture of the first days:

> Though the building was far from complete, classes were scheduled to begin on October 1. On the previous Monday, a bitter cold day, the Sisters met the students in front of the building to take orders for books and to impart any desired information.
>
> Informal groups of brightly clad girls and somberly dressed nuns chatted and shivered in the frosty morning air, while inside the building busy workmen sawed and planed, hammered and drilled, in a mad endeavor to have sufficient number of rooms ready to admit the students the following week (p. 357).

With the inconveniences of construction behind them, Grace, together with the faculty and students, concentrated on making Regina High School into an exemplary educational institution. By providing both knowledge and practice in religion, academics, and social development, the school laid a thorough foundation for the future lives of the students. When Grace left Regina ten years later in 1938, the school possessed a solid reputation for excellence.

Wapakoneta, Ohio

Grace's next assignment took her to St. Joseph High School in Wapakoneta, Ohio, a school in existence since 1908. Grace moved with apparent ease from a new school to a very old one, from an all-girls' school to a co-educational institution, from an urban to a rural economy. As she assumed direction of St. Joseph's, she went about making it a better place by initiating up-to-date teaching methods, installing new equipment and training instructors in modern methods.

Grace's influence at St. Joseph's is described in a letter from a former student, Raymond Hammer from Huntington, Indiana, on the occasion of her 100th birthday in 1978:

> It was with absolute joy that I received a copy of an article in the June 2 issue of the *Catholic Telegraph* regarding your 100th birthday. My belated congratulations on this historic event—and we who are fortunate enough to have been touched by your presence are grateful that you were afforded these many years to expand the scope of your influence. . . .
>
> You became principal of St. Joseph [High] School the year I started my senior year. You tutored me in mathematics. What you were able to teach me gave me an unfair advantage over my peers when I later went to college. . . .
>
> Sister, you taught me so much more than just mathematics. In my own career as an engineer, I spent nine years teaching thermodynamics and heat transfer. To the very limit of my ability, I tried to emulate you. Your scope of influence has been multiplied by those of us who had the good fortune to have been your students. . . .

Grace's reputation as a school architect and designer attracted national recognition. In 1948 she presented a paper in Chicago at the First National Catholic Building Convention and Exposition. As part of a panel, listed as "The Sisters' Viewpoint," she and other sisters described for architects and school superintendents how important the function of a building must be in its construction. Grace articulated her life-long conviction that environment contributed to the quality of learning. A few quotes from her no-nonsense presentation shed light on the practical implications of her beliefs:

> *We shall begin our discussion with the classroom. The walls and the ceiling should, if possible, have a coat or covering of acoustical material. . . . This prevents echoes and both pupils and teacher may speak in moderate tone and still be understood; thus the energy of both is, to a great extent, conserved. . . .*
>
> *Although the windows do not strictly come under equipment since they are part of the building, nevertheless they are also of great importance to the teachers. Two things should be kept in mind when installing them: First, the kind selected should be such that they can be opened without causing a direct current of air to strike the children. Second, that they may be opened in such a way as to enable the janitor to clean the exterior of the windows from the inside of the room. This eliminates the use of outside scaffolds or ladders. . . .*

Grace continued in that vein, reviewing all the particulars that should be included in the planning and construction of a school. Focusing on a modern high school, she spoke of the need to have fully functioning science labs, an auditorium, an art room, a music department, rooms for commercial studies, home economics, mechanical drawing, and a cafeteria. She also spelled out the need for a gymnasium with showers and equipment rooms. Outlining the necessary contents in a high school library, she even said how high windows should be for optimum light and for circulation. She closed her paper with *a word on color scheme: The desks, tables, and other equipment should all be in harmony with the wood finish of the room. Medium light colors are always preferable to dark.* She had something to say about every facet of school construction. Shortly after the presentation of this paper on June 30, 1948, Grace was elected to the General Council of the Sisters of the Precious Blood.

Grace on the Council

In the Congregational election of 1948, Sister Nathalia Smith was elected as the mother superior with Sisters Celeste Grimmelsman, Simplicia McGreevy, Grace, and Aquinas Stadtherr as councilors. While she was a member of the Council, Grace also taught math to novices in the Salem Heights college department. One novice commented, "I never liked math—couldn't understand algebra—until Grace taught me. Her evident love of the subject made the material so simple that I began having fun solving equations."

Shortly after her election, Mother Nathalia began planning for the construction of two buildings on the motherhouse grounds. The first was a high school for young girls aspiring to enter religious life. Grace was an active participant in all facets of the planning and was instrumental in making Fatima Hall, which opened in 1950, a modern high school building. Prior to this time, aspirants had been housed in the novitiate wing of the motherhouse. The new structure provided spacious living quarters and academic surroundings.

Almost immediately after the completion of Fatima Hall, Mother Nathalia moved forward on the construction of Lourdes Hall, a nursing care facility for elderly and infirm members of the Congregation. Grace once again shared her expertise in planning and in the drawing of blueprints. Much of what she had learned through working with school construction, was applicable in this project. Recognizing and respecting her knowledge and experience, the architect and the construction crew accepted her input.

Maria Joseph Home for the Aged

In 1953, another Congregational need prompted superiors to call upon the multi-talented and totally responsible Grace once again. The Maria Joseph Home for the Aged, the construction of which Grace had influenced, was receiving an increased number of applicants. Society had become more accepting of families placing elderly and infirm parents and grandparents in health care facilities where they could receive professional care. Because the postwar economy was booming, more families could afford nursing home accommodations for their loved ones. As a result, the demand for nursing homes dramatically increased.

The Maria Joseph Home that had opened in 1930 possessed a fine reputation. However, only two of the originally planned wings were completed, and very little had been done to improve the building during the 20 years since its opening. The Great Depression had curtailed spending, and materials were difficult to obtain during the following war years. The relative affluence of the 1950s made it possible at last to update the facility.

Maria Joseph Home

By 1953 the Maria Joseph Home had a long waiting list of applicants. Sister Annetta Schneider had been administrator since 1950. Her outstanding love and care for the residents no doubt contributed to the need for additional rooms. Annetta's heart, however, was in the West where she had spent 50 years of ministry. When she returned to California in 1953, the Maria Joseph Home was in need of a new administrator. Grace, though 75 years old and still serving on the Council, was called upon once again. *More Than the Doing*, by Janet Davis Richardson CSJP and Canice Werner CPPS, describes how she took hold of this new challenge:

A mathematician and an experienced high school administrator . . . Sister Grace recognized the needs at Maria Joseph Home for the Aged as being in two areas: the finances and the physical plant. The job of meeting these needs became hers when she was appointed the administrator. She was determined to make the Home financially viable. As Councilor she pushed for the addition that had been proposed during Mother Magna's term. To help finance it, the Council voted and got permission to sell some community land in Dayton which was not being farmed and was not accruing income to the Congregation (p. 137).

The Chapter of 1954 elected Sister Aquinas Stadtherr to lead the Congregation and placed many demands on the new administration. Although no longer a member of the Council, Grace unflinchingly presented her plans for the expansion of the Maria Joseph Home. She maintained that it was time to finish the building as it was originally designed. Three wings, including additional guest rooms and other facilities previously unheard of in nursing homes, were yet to be completed. She proposed a large chapel, an auditorium for social and cultural events, and a pleasant dining room with an up-to-date kitchen.

Events moved quickly, and already on October 7, 1954, groundbreaking for the chapel wing, the first wing to be added, took place. The following spring on March 24, both the *Catholic Telegraph Register* and the *Dayton Daily News* covered the laying of the cornerstone. A front-page article in the *News* told the story of a bequest of $200,000 to the Home from the estate of John Westendorf whose wife had been one of the leaders in promoting the Home in the 1920s. The first Mass in the new chapel was celebrated on Christmas Day, 1955. In April of 1957, the Council approved plans for construction of the remaining two wings of the building, and these were completed in 1960. The final structure gave abundant evidence of Grace's expert touch—a combination of beauty and function.

Grace also addressed the challenge of inadequate finances. The sale of properties, gifts and bequests provided most of the $567,347, the total cost of the 1954-1960 additions. But the institution's operating costs, subsidized by the Congregation for many years, also needed to be addressed. Grace, vigorously but fairly, solved this problem by designing and implementing a realistic financial plan to make the Home self-supporting.

In 1959, Grace's six years as superior at Maria Joseph Home, the canonical limit for a superior's term, came to an end. Since Mother Aquinas regarded Grace's services as indispensable, she obtained permission from Rome to extend her administration until the building projects and the complete implementation of sound fiscal policies were accomplished. Grace continued as administrator and superior until 1963. After that time, she remained at Maria Joseph Home as bookkeeper until she retired in 1967.

Grace's last years

In 1967 at age 89, Grace retired from active service and moved to Lourdes Hall. She lived on for another 12 years, spending her time in prayer and enjoying some well-earned leisure. Grace exceeded the age of most of her contemporaries, celebrating her 75th, 80th and 85th jubilees in the Congregation. Remaining alert and able to communicate, she was able to participate in a small party marking her 100th birthday in May, 1978. The following year on November 11, 1979, Grace died from the complications of old age. She had lived 101 years and had spent a record 86 of them in the Congregation.

Grace is remembered for a great deal more than her longevity. She was a conscientious, hard working woman who willingly and generously shared her many skills. She was a teacher, a school administrator, a mathematician, an architect and a financier. She spent years as administrator of schools, and later, of a home for the aged. For over 25 years she was superior in the convents where she lived. Mother superiors sought her counsel. Business men and construction workers were in awe of her abilities. Most of all, perhaps, Grace was a faithful religious who devoted 86 years of her life to the service of God.

A person visiting Salem Heights today, enters the same building where Grace spent a great deal of her creative energies. The five-winged building, formerly the Maria Joseph Home for the Aged, is now the new Salem Heights, the home for retired Sisters of the Precious Blood. Because of Grace and her vision, sisters living there experience a pleasant and user-friendly environment—the unity of beauty and function that she sought.

A few years ago, sisters, seeking a name for a large multi-function room on the lower level off the rotunda in Salem Heights, agreed that no other name but "Grace Hall" would be appropriate. This designation is a small but significant reminder of the respect and affection with which they remember their energetic and talented sister.

Sister Friedburga (Maria) Jaeger (1894-1969)

By Eleanor McNally CPPS

With their eyes peering intently and their hearts racing, 22 excited Jaeger relatives waited expectantly in the airline terminal in Stuttgart, Germany. Would they be able to recognize the three sisters—Rudolpha, Friedburga and Renata—who, each in her own time many years before, had tearfully left the family in Tettnang? Each had taken the long journey across the Atlantic on the Red Star Line Steamer, which brought the sisters separately to New York. From there, each had traveled overland to Maria Stein, Ohio, where she entered the Community of the Sisters of the Precious Blood.

Ever since the Pan American plane left Idlewild Airport in New York at 4:30 p.m. on a brisk February day in 1955, the hearts of the sisters were overflowing with anticipation. During the flight they had time to think about the years since they had left their home and to thank God for guidance through times of sorrow and of joy. Friedburga smiled to herself, and the candle of love in her heart burned brighter. This is the story of how she kept that flame burning throughout her life.

Beginnings

Maria Jaeger came into the life of Anton Jaeger and Josepha Lansenberger on April 11, 1894. The family was large—three boys and five girls. Maria, Anton's inseparable companion, was known as "her father's girl." As strong as this bond was, Maria was willing to sacrifice it in response to the call to religious life. In discerning which religious community to enter, Maria had one non-negotiable item on her list. She did not want to go to a "begging" community!

In May of 1906, Maria left Tettnang, her home town in Germany, for the convent of the Sisters of the Precious Blood in Maria Stein, Ohio. Although she would find her sister, Josephine (now Sister Rudolpha), at the convent when she arrived, it still took considerable courage to leave home at the age of 12! Because she was too young to enter the postulancy, she was sent to the boarding school in Minster operated by the sisters where the tears of the homesick little girl could be dried by a loving nun.

Four years later on May 30, 1910, at the age of 16, Maria entered the Congregation. Her novitiate began the following year, and on August 15, 1913, she made temporary vows. Her sister Anna (later Renata), who had arrived from Tettnang the previous day, was on hand to witness Maria (now Friedburga) receive the black veil. What a joyful reunion! Sixteen-year-old Anna brought with her from Germany the loving spiritual presence of their mother and father, and the brothers and sisters they thought they would never see again.

After profession, Friedburga attended the Normal School at Maria Stein for one year. In 1914 she was missioned to teach at St. Joseph's School in Wapakoneta, Ohio just as World War I was beginning. Undoubtedly, the next four years were difficult for this young woman from Germany. She worried about her family in her homeland, and at the same time, she was often looked upon with suspicion by some Americans. The result of this personal turmoil was the beginning of an intimate relationship with God lasting through her long and fruitful life.

She was assigned to St. Barbara's School in Cloverdale, Ohio in 1918, the year of the devastating epidemic of Spanish influenza. She and the other sisters spent days and nights consoling stricken families whose loved ones had succumbed to this fatal disease. This powerful experience surely helped her recognize her own gift of compassion. Beyond teaching, she was destined for an apostolate of caring for those who suffer, a trait that would endear her to countless persons throughout her life.

St. Joseph's Orphanage
When Friedburga was assigned in 1919 to St. Joseph's Orphanage in Dayton, Ohio, the institution had been in existence for 70 years. Founded in 1849 by lay persons, it offered

a haven for children whose parents had been victims of cholera, for orphans of the poor, and for destitute children needing help and guidance.

This orphanage, the "oldest charitable institution in Dayton," was entrusted to the Sisters of the Precious Blood in 1891. During Friedburga's time at the orphanage, its name was changed to St. Joseph's Home for Children. By mid-20th century, many of the boys and girls at the Home were not orphans. Often they came from one-parent homes or from homes unable to nurture children. At St. Joseph's, Friedburga found children yearning for love and for some semblance of stability in their lives.

The sisters at St. Joseph's cared deeply for the boys and girls entrusted to them. They strove to develop in the children a sense of self-worth and to give them tools with which to succeed in the adult world. Friedburga was assigned to mentor the older boys with whom she immediately established good rapport. Perhaps growing up in a large family had prepared her for this challenging labor of love. The sisters did everything they could to make the Home the best possible substitute for the families the children were missing.

On the occasion of the 100th anniversary of the founding of St. Joseph's (1949), the *Dayton Daily News* gave three columns to the story of the Home. Following are a few excerpts:

> In the family home the lively youngster comes roaring in from school, slamming doors and yelling for something to eat. At St. Joseph's, the patient nuns are on hand to greet their charges when they come from school, and the children pause only long enough to playfully cuff "Roughy" or "Flash"—their two dogs, before descending upon the trays of doughnuts or jam and butter bread held by the nuns. . . . This child needs a glass of extra fortified milk, and that one cut his finger playing in the school yard. They scamper away to the Cottage, an infirmary in miniature, immaculately clean, where the nun ministers to their demands, real or even sometimes fancied. . . .

Friedburga's gentle love and motherliness contributed to the warm atmosphere of the Home. The ever-expanding interests of each child became important components of preparation for their lives as adults.

Accidents will happen

On a hot July day in 1927, the boys from St. Joseph's Home were playing baseball, with Friedburga on the sidelines cheering them on. With permission of the St. Louis Cardinals baseball team, that had taken a special interest in the boys at the Home, the boys wore the Cardinals' logo. Suddenly, a well-hit ball fouled into the sidelines. As Friedburga tried desperately to shield the younger children, the ball struck her full force in her left eye shattering her glasses.

Severely injured, she was rushed to St. Elizabeth Hospital where she lingered between life and death for weeks. Thanks to the prayers of the sisters and the children, she was able to return to the orphanage on August 20. However, as a result of the accident, she suffered very painful headaches for 14 years. Eventually, she consented to have her eye replaced with a plastic one. Friedburga refused to lay blame for the accident or to complain about her pain. Her boys were very upset by the unfortunate incident, and through the years they continued to "touch base" with her over and over again until her dying day.

Superior at St. Joseph's

In 1936 Friedburga became superior at St. Joseph's Home. She was now "mother," not only to the boys, but also to the girls and to the sisters as well. She was never too busy or too tired to greet everyone with a smile and a kind word. Sister Eleanor McNally, who worked at the Home for several summers during the war years, writes of her:

> She was a rare superior for those days, one who really loved and trusted each of the sisters. I remember being so impressed with her thoughtfulness. As superior she kept the convent rule of opening each

Sister Friedburga (Maria) Jaeger

sister's mail, but she slit the envelope only half an inch. The privacy of our mail was assured, and yet she had done her duty. Smart lady! She was always pleasant, understanding and long-suffering.

Friedburga was a remarkable administrator. Running a home for disadvantaged children necessitated good public relations and expertise in dealing with civic and state authorities, as well as with local business persons. Delicate negotiations with parents and guardians, who sometimes did not have the best interests of the child at heart, were a constant necessity. With the boys and girls, Friedburga's fairness was laced with deep compassion. She exercised a caring discipline that molded the young people into independent adults. Years later, when former students, now in stable marriages, brought their children to visit her, she enjoyed the rewards of her efforts.

World War II

Although born in Germany, Friedburga's love for her adopted country was deep and sincere. Sisters recall the beautiful scene at St. Joseph's when the superior would lower the American flag at sundown and reverently fold it as something precious and dear. Friedburga loved her God, her adopted country, and all with whom she lived and worked. She did not, however, forget her native land and her own family who were suffering in Germany. When Putnam County in northern Ohio mobilized to send care packages to loved ones in Europe, Friedburga went to Glandorf to explain how to pack supplies, how to sew money into clothing hems, and how to code letters to alert recipients. Because common sense was one of Friedburga's virtues, human love and caring often took precedence over legal considerations.

God closes one door . . .

When Friedburga's time at St. Joseph's came to a close, she looked back on some of her experiences there. In her first year, fire had destroyed the upper story of the barn; in 1939 the swimming pool was opened; and in 1944 the small log cabin party room for the children was built. In 1949 she had worked with 1200 volunteers on the annual picnic. Many of the 50,000 in attendance had been children at the Home who were loved into responsible adulthood by Friedburga and the other sisters. She had encouraged young journalists as they prepared copy for the Home's newsletter, *The Hillside*. She had developed fiscal responsibility by encouraging each child to build up his/her own bank account in the bank established at the Home.

Friedburga believed that development of the children's prayer life was vital. She loved the singing of the children in the chapel: the little ones with their sweet clear voices and the eighth grade boys giving volume and depth in their developing grown-up voices. John Burman, who had spent his childhood at St. Joseph's Home, said, "When I travel down the 'Memory Lane' of my life, I always end up thinking that there is no amount of gold or no station in life that I would accept for the four years that I spent with the Sisters of the Precious Blood at the Orphanage." Of the 200 sisters who altogether gave a thousand years of service to the children of Dayton, none was more devoted than Friedburga.

... and opens another

In 1949 Friedburga was called to another part of the Lord's vineyard. In mileage, Maria Stein is not far from Dayton, but it was a world away for the kind nun whose loving smile and caring heart would now be given to a whole new group of God's people. She moved from the laughter of children to the concerns of adults; from a bustling city to the tiniest of hamlets; from busy streets with screaming fire engines to a peaceful countryside where only the sound of church bells would break the morning stillness. In Mercer County's farmlands, Friedburga became superior of the sisters and administrator of the Shrine of the Holy Relics.

Pilgrims traveled to the Shrine at Maria Stein for a closer contact with saints who once walked this earth. The story of how this unusually large collection of relics eventually found a home at Maria Stein in 1872 is interesting. In mid-19th century, the Italian banditti stole many relics from the European churches with an eye to making money from them. Eventually, Reverend J. M. Gartner, a Missionary of the Sacred Heart from Milwaukee, came into possession of the relics. In his search for the best place to house them, he heard about Maria Stein. Gartner decided to place the relics in the trust of the Maria Stein sisters for two reasons: 1) he valued the Perpetual Adoration of the Blessed Sacrament carried on by the sisters, and 2) he considered Mercer County to be the "Holy Land" of America.

Responding to the spirituality of the day, the sisters opened the Shrine to pilgrims. Friedburga was a gracious hostess to many people from far and near. They came by foot, by car, and by bus to renew their spirituality through devotion to the saints. The Knights of St. John frequently sponsored the World Peace Pilgrimage at the Relic Chapel where untold numbers of people experienced Friedburga's beautiful smile and her hospitality. Often they even attributed God's healing powers to her loving intercession *(Our Lady of the Rock Newsletter,* April 1976).

Work on the convent

When Friedburga became superior and administrator, the Maria Stein convent was 110 years old. It had been built around 1840 shortly after the removal of the last Shawnee Indians from the territory and the completion of the Miami-Erie Canal. Because of its age, the building needed considerable repair. Friedburga lost no time in putting her astute business sense to work to transform the convent into a pilgrim-friendly place. A patio adjacent to the chapel became a sidewalk cafe edged with a garden of flowers. Opposite the chapel a door led to the coffee shop, formerly the old kitchen. Fourth floor rooms were beautified for retreatants, and laundry

Friedburga holds a model of the Maria Stein Retreat House.

equipment was installed. A new kitchen and dining room followed. The relics were refurbished and new ones acquired.

Outside, the Shrine of the Woods was repaired and rustic fences were built around wooded areas. The courtyard was completely redone. Through donations, Friedburga began to erect statues at various spots on the grounds. And the pilgrims kept coming. A local paper in 1953 recorded the following: "Now in their growing convent in the quiet countryside here, the Sisters are conducting retreats and days of recollection for women." The time was ripe for expanding.

Retreat House dreams

By 1953 the Congregation had built two very large additions to the Salem Heights convent: Fatima Hall for incoming candidates and Lourdes Hall for retired and infirm sisters. Consequently, the Community had no money to finance improvements at Maria Stein. Dark days seemed to lie ahead for the Shrine. Friedburga, once the little 12-year-old girl who did not want to join a "begging" community, found herself begging anyway. At St. Joseph's, she had asked for money because she loved the children; she would do it now for the sake of those who yearned to enrich their spiritual lives.

There was not enough room at Maria Stein for the many men, women, youth groups, organizations and others who sought time out for retreats and days of recollection. The time had come to consider building a retreat house. Thus began the endless round of card parties, garden parties, and festivals that would be the prime sources of income. Eventually, Friedburga would have to make a public appeal for funds to help build the new retreat house. She gently but persuasively urged friends and Shrine supporters to help her realize her dream. Who could resist that humble, beautiful smile and the obvious love she felt for the people?

In 1954 Mother Nathalia Smith, the dreamer and planner, joined Friedburga at Maria Stein. The latter was already involved with the Lay Women's Retreat Movement, and she welcomed an enthusiastic new colleague. The Maria Stein Retreat League originated in 1956, and already by 1959, it was so successful that its president, Clementine Stein, was elected to the National Lay Retreat League. With Friedburga, Mother Nathalia and Clementine, determined and hard-working women, the dream of a Maria Stein Retreat House would become a reality.

On May 1, 1960, ground was broken, and on September 3, 1962, the new facility was ready for its first retreat. The *Maria Stein News Letter* included the following: "From the humble beginnings of Shrine facilities to the completion of the present Maria Stein Retreat House, she [Friedburga] was the guiding force, the faithful source of encouragement, hope, trust and confidence that surmounted the many trying problems."

A trip home

With the Retreat House well on its way, it was time for Friedburga and her sisters, Rudolpha and Renata, to journey to their homeland. The Assembly of 1954 had given sisters from foreign countries permission to visit their countries of origin. Although the parents of the Jaeger sisters were deceased, other relatives still lived in Germany. So the three of them traveled to Tettnang, the city in Germany each had left so many years before. After their arrival in Germany, Friedburga wrote:

> *A three hour auto ride brought us to Tettnang, our home, and to the very house in which we had parted from our parents so long ago. The first few days were spent in getting acquainted with our dear ones and speaking of all that had happened since we left. Our Parish Church had been bombed during the second World War, the sanctuary and choir being partially destroyed. This was rebuilt and redecorated in time for our arrival. Our first Sunday Mass there was a great joy. It was celebrated with special pomp; fourteen servers were in the sanctuary and a mixed choir sang beautifully.*

After visiting the surrounding area, the sisters traveled to Rome where they were spiritually rejuvenated in this city so rich in tradition. Then they returned to their little German village for a few more days of reminiscing about the past and enjoying their beloved family members. Friedburga later wrote, *At the airport in Stuttgart, many of our closest relatives accompanied us to see us off. As the plane took flight they waved and many tears were shed.* Friedburga, always appreciative, ended her account with thanks to *our superiors and friends for making this trip possible.*

Remembering

Friedburga returned to her baptismal name of Maria in 1967. She bore the name for only two years before she died, not quite long enough for those who knew her to become accustomed to it. Their memories of her, however, are many. Sister Agnes Christine Mullen remembers her as a "humble sister, but a very outgoing person both to our sisters and also to lay people. She listened to people and was very understanding and very gracious and generous with her time. [She was] a very prayerful person too."

The laity were no less impressed. One of her many friends said:

> To me Sister Friedburga was a woman of God. She was never too busy nor too tired to greet you with a smile and a kind word. How great was her love of Nature and all of its glories! I cannot help but think how often she repeated the prayer, "God, we give You thanks for all your great glories" *(Maria Stein Newsletter).*

A beautiful plaque graces the entrance to Maria Stein. It reads, "In memory of Sister Mary Friedburga Jaeger, CPPS, 1894 - 1969. In loving memory of Sister Friedburga for her dedicated service to the Maria Stein Community, this plaque is erected through the generosity of her many friends." Friedburga inspired others with her own deep piety. In 1969, The *CPPS Dialog* said of her, "For those who came to Maria

29

Stein, she was a source of strength, comfort, peace and joy. She was also a clear-headed business woman and a tender mother to those in trouble."

Maria Stein Convent around 1910

The candle flickers

Life came to a close for Friedburga on March 8, 1969. She had contracted malignant cancer and suffered intensely during her last days. A touching account of her final days was written by Sister Rosemary Raney in a piece entitled "Her Last Smile." According to her account, a few evenings before her death, Friedburga held out her hands and pleaded, "Help me! Help me! My God, heal me!" Frequently on her lips was the simple word of her childhood, "Mama!" As Rosemary recited the prayers for the dying, she dwelt affectionately on the name of Jesus. The second time she said "Jesus," Friedburga opened her good eye wide. Rosemary writes:

> . . . and in that eye and on her lips was "The Smile" I'll never forget. It lasted for only a few seconds. Then she took one long breath. All was so quiet

for a few seconds that it seemed an eternity to me. There was still a faint pulse and then she exhaled deeply. By this time I am sure she was in the arms of Jesus. Her life-time prayer was to be the hidden violet of Jesus and always to be joyful, no matter what God asked.

Friedburga's life was likened to a candle "consumed before the face of Christ." Her accomplishments, however, caused her to seem more like a torch, a glowing fire. At the hour of her death, some sisters reported seeing a spectacular display of light. At the same moment that Friedburga passed into eternity, sisters praying the night hour before the Blessed Sacrament at Maria Stein witnessed brilliant flashing amber and pink reflections on the new-fallen snow outside the chapel window. It might have been simply the snapping of a high tension line against a transformer pole. However, many saw it as the candle of Friedburga's life cascading into brilliant light.

It is believed that when a medicine man goes to the top of the mountain to initiate a young boy, one can see from far away the flashes of light as the power of the Spirit beautifies the skies. It is not impossible that Friedburga's gentle steady candle burned itself out in a blaze of heavenly glory.

Sister Claire Trimbach (1914-1983)

By Rose Margaret Broerman CPPS

Darkness had descended on Salem Heights Convent. Its long corridors were faintly illuminated, but the stillness of the December night was pregnant with expectation. Faint strains of music began to break the silence and gradually swelled into the familiar melody of "Silent Night." The plaintive sound of a single violin wafted through the hallways.

Sister Mary Claire Trimbach once again was awakening the Community and inviting its members to rise for Midnight Mass. Soon the corridors were filled with sisters, novices and postulants hurrying to chapel for the festive celebration. Having completed her rounds, the petite nun laid aside her violin and moved to the organ bench. Soon the chapel resounded with majestic organ music and the clear voices of the sisters.

Background

Rita Trimbach was born to Jennie Rennie and Leo J. Trimbach on March 8, 1914 in Dayton, Ohio. She had three siblings—two brothers and a sister. Taught by Precious Blood

Sister Claire Trimbach

sisters at St. Mary's School, Rita studied piano and violin at the convent. According to Sister Beatrice Marie (Mary Elizabeth) Hafer, Rita was recruited in junior high by her music teacher, Sister Stephana Kamp, to play the violin with a small ensemble of talented youth. Besides Rita, the group included Mary Elizabeth Hafer from St. Joseph Orphanage who played the trumpet, and Beatrice (Paula Marie) Will who played trombone. They performed for church functions and for various occasions. Every Saturday morning the group met for practice at St. Mary's Convent.

At the age of 16, Rita responded to the Lord's call to religious life. On September 7, 1930 she joined the aspirancy (high school) at Salem Heights Convent in her home town where she completed her high school education. She was often found in the music rooms, practicing piano under the tutelage of Sister Prisca Simbeck who became a life-long friend.

Upon entrance into the novitiate, Rita received the name, Sister Mary Claire. Recognized early on for her musical talent, while still a novice she gave music lessons to neighboring school children. Together with Sisters Roselma Foos and Palmira (Paula Marie) Will, Claire often delighted in providing entertainment for the novices on feast days.

Following her first profession on August 15, 1933, Claire began a long and distinguished career as a music educator. This tiny woman exuded quiet charm and graciousness, as well as a professionalism that stood her in good stead through the next 50 years. She possessed a wonderful smile and a delightful sense of humor. Though cheerful by nature, she had a no-nonsense approach to teaching. Whether on her way to chapel, to her music rooms, or to community activities, her determined walk revealed that she meant business.

Claire attended the Athenaeum of Ohio in Cincinnati where she received her bachelor's degree in music education in 1952, with a major in violin and a minor in organ. In 1960 she earned a master's degree in musicology from the Conservatory of Music in Cincinnati. Though she was very accomplished on both the organ and the piano, her favorite instrument was the violin. Sister Mary Linus Bax said "Claire made the violin speak."

Claire's mission assignments from 1934 to 1945 took her to Regina High School in Norwood, Ohio, to Our Lady of Good Counsel in Cleveland, and to St. Mark's in Cincinnati. During these years she taught both piano and instrumental music. In Cleveland (1941-1945), she offered to teach piano to the sisters with whom she lived. Since, at that time, every classroom had a piano, sisters could practice whenever they had the opportunity. While none of them became skilled musicians, all were pleased to have learned some piano basics. This group enjoyed giving monthly recitals for the other sisters at Good Counsel. In Cleveland, she also invited some of her friends from the Cleveland Conservatory to the convent to entertain the sisters.

Liturgical awareness

For most of the years from 1945 to 1968, Claire ministered at Salem Heights. During these important years, she exercised a major role in educating the Congregation in greater liturgical awareness. She was responsible for the preparation of all liturgies, feast days, processions and vespers. Many a sister can trace her introduction to and her love for Gregorian chant to Claire and her assistants during these years.

Working closely with Dr. Francois LeFevre, a guest from France of the Trappists in Kentucky, Claire educated the Community on the fine points of Gregorian chant. In November, 1951, the Salem Heights community sang plain chant vespers for the first time. Under her instruction, the chanting of the office became reverent and prayerful. Claire often stood in the middle aisle of chapel to direct the singing of vespers. After the sisters became proficient, she did this only when the community needed a reminder to keep the chanting at a slower, more prayerful pace. Sister Maureen Mangen recalls how she loved when Claire played soft accompaniment during Sunday and feast day vespers. "It always felt so prayerful and almost heavenly. Even when vespers were long, I didn't want them to end." Maureen remembers that

Claire at the organ directs the novices in the Salem Hights Chapel.

Claire was a "one-of-a-kind" musician and teacher. She adds, "Claire played the organ with hands and feet going 60 miles an hour while directing the choir. Yet she never seemed to 'lose her cool.'"

In addition to her liturgical responsibilities, Claire gave private organ, piano, and violin lessons to the novices and postulants. She formed and directed the choir and glee club at Salem Heights. The choir was composed of novices and junior professed; aspirants and postulants formed the glee club. Under her direction, these choral groups made a recording entitled "Lift Up Your Hearts." The choir rendered the sacred music, including "Veni Sponsa Christi," "Ave Maria," "Pater Noster," and "Confirma Hoc," on Side A. All of these motets were composed specifically for the choir. The aspirants and postulants recorded secular songs on Side B. Among those included were "The Sound of Music," "You'll Never Walk Alone," and "Over the Rainbow."

Meeting Perry Como

A favorite anecdote about Claire was the story of her encounter with the famous singer, Perry Como. One day in Cincinnati she was shopping for sheet music at the Willis

Music Company. Approaching her with a tall handsome stranger, the manager introduced her to Perry Como, commenting that his children were in a Catholic school. Claire, being unfamiliar with the name, inquired, "Oh, are you interested in music?" Needless to say, when she shared this story with others, she received a great deal of teasing. Being very good-natured, she enjoyed the joke on herself.

A labor of love for Claire was the compilation of the brown *Community Hymnal*. Claire and other music instructors at the Motherhouse selected the songs for this hymnal compiled solely for use in CPPS convent chapels. Permission to use some of the hymns was given with the understanding that the books would not be used in parish churches, schools or other institutions. A few hymns which might seem to violate the liturgical spirit were included because of their traditional appeal within the Community.

Claire handwrote the melody lines for all the songs. This hymnal became the basis for songs used during Hours of

Claire in the grey habit

Adoration, Benediction, Eucharistic celebrations, processions, etc. Some of the songs were reserved for special feasts and other solemn occasions. This hymnal is the source for many Community favorites still sung today, especially "Glory Be to Jesus" and "Blood of Jesus, Strength of Martyrs."

A memorable trip

Sister Madonna Winkeljohn remembers the summer Sisters Claire, Mildred Gutman and Mildred's sister, Sister Eloise SC and she drove to California so that the Gutman sisters could visit family. Sister Alma Catherine Huelskamp, who was on her way to Denver, also accompanied them. Having planned the trip carefully, the sisters usually stopped at convents overnight, either with Precious Blood sisters or with Sisters of Charity.

Along the road in Arizona, they were amused by various signs such as: "This is the last stop before entering the desert!" and "Watch for flash floods!" What, they asked one another, were they to do if a flash flood did occur? Some cold water might have been appreciated since the car was not air-conditioned, and the weather was HOT!

While still in Arizona, they stopped for gas in a very small town. Studying the map, they noticed that one route looked much shorter than the one they were currently using. The station attendant assured them, "Yes, it would be shorter." Reassured, they decided to take it, and what an experience it turned out to be! The road had sudden drop-offs, it was often too narrow to pass on-coming vehicles, and they had to negotiate scary curves! The travelers offered many a fervent prayer along the way. It seems the sisters had taken the famous (infamous) Apache Trail! Through it all, Claire had a calming effect on the Gutman sisters. This travel adventure provided the sisters with many memories to share over the years.

Making new melodies

Claire ended her career in music education in Minster, Ohio. From 1968 to 1983, she gave private lessons and taught music in the Minster Public School. In the early months of 1983, however, Claire began to experience brief black-out periods. Sadly, tests eventually revealed that she had a brain tumor. It was this condition that led to her retirement in June, 1983. At a party in her honor, she received a plaque from the Minster Teachers' Association to mark the end of her career as an outstanding music educator.

In September 1983, Claire became a resident at Emma Hall. There she continued her life-long task of making beautiful melodies for others to enjoy. But now her tunes were no longer musical. Instead, her reassuring words and her gentle witness created melodies in the hearts and lives of others. Writing to Claire during this period, Becky Honeycutt, her care-giver, shared some of her reflections: "You always wanted to help everyone, no matter how great the task. Some days we would come in and be kinda down, but you always sensed this and would somehow know the right thing to say to us. It always came straight from your heart."

Claire answered her *Veni, Sponsa Christi* call from the Lord on December 12, 1983. A part of the eulogy in her Resurrection Liturgy follows:

> . . . Sister Claire was music teacher, choir director, and gentle inspiration to postulants, novices and sisters at the motherhouse for 22 years. The many among us who knew, loved and were influenced by her, treasure precious memories. Organ peals, festive songs at Christmas Midnight Mass, and melodies from August 15th profession liturgies still ring. . . .

Sister Amabilis Neumeister (1894 -1970)
By Eleanor McNally CPPS

Anyone entering the tiny office of Sister Amabilis Neumeister, treasurer general of the Sisters of the Precious Blood from1944 to 1966, faced a dizzying sight: stacks of paper here, piles of booklets there, drawers and files overflowing, shelves bulging with apparently unorganized data, and an old-fashioned roll-top desk perched in the midst of it all.

Sister Mary Linus Bax, former Congregational archivist, characterized Amabilis, the sole occupant of this domain, as having "an ability to manage chaos in terms that did not seem to have any potential for order." Even so, a person requesting anything from the amiable treasurer, from train schedules to multi-million dollar deeds to properties, waited only a few seconds till her hands went directly to the desired object. Her extraordinary mind and totally unorthodox organizational skills, along with a work ethic that never stopped, combined to make Amabilis both an extraordinary woman and an excellent treasurer of the Congregation.

Cincinnati native

The first child of Joseph and Theresa Miller Neumeister, Anna Mary was born in the family home in Cincinnati, Ohio on March 25, 1894. Joseph, who was a shoemaker, had emigrated from Bavaria, Germany; Theresa came from Egg Harbor, New Jersey. In the course of time, a daughter (name unknown) and three sons—Carl, Joseph, and George—were added to the family, all of whom lived in or around Cincinnati most of their lives.

Less than two weeks after her birth, Anna Mary was baptized at St. George's Church, 42 Calhoun Street, in Cincinnati. Years later, the Athenaeum of Ohio, where many Precious Blood sisters received their first college degrees, would be located adjacent to the church. While Anna Mary was still a child, the family moved to Evanston, a Cincinnati suburb, where they joined St. Mark's Parish, and the children began their education at the parish school. The Most Rev. Henry

41

Moeller, Archbishop of Cincinnati, confirmed Anna when she was 12 years old.

Although the family became well-acquainted with the Sisters of the Precious Blood who conducted the school, Anna's call to religious life did not come in her early years. After elementary school she went to high school, and later attended Miller School of Business from which she graduated around 1914. She then immersed herself in the business world, little dreaming that someday this experience would enable a large institution with many members and many properties to stay afloat financially.

The Call

Thirteen years later, Anna discerned and responded to the call to religious life. No written records exist revealing any struggle she may have had in deciding to respond to the invitation of Christ. Perhaps her delay in entering until she was 33 was prompted by a need to help her family. All that is known is that one day in 1927 she asked the pastor of St. Mark's, Father Mark Hamburger CPPS, for a recommendation to the Sisters of the Precious Blood in Dayton, Ohio. His letter says in part:

> To whom it may concern:
> These lines introduce to you Miss Anna Neumeister, an estimable young lady who went through St. Mark's School, received her First Holy Communion here and was confirmed at St. Mark's. She is a virtuous and studious young lady, always held in the highest esteem, and [I] can conscientiously recommend her as a fit applicant for the life she wishes to embrace as a religious.

When Anna entered the postulancy on August 15,1927, the Salem Heights motherhouse in Dayton, Ohio, was only four years old. Vocations were plentiful and her class was large. At age 33, she may have stood out a bit from the rest of the young women, since most of the postulants were considerably younger. Nevertheless, with her quiet and docile manner, she fit in well. Like others joining the convent in those days, she quickly faded into the anonymity characterizing this life of detachment and silence. After a year, her class of 34 young women entered the novitiate, and Anna received the religious name, Sister Mary Amabilis.

A variety of activities designed to prepare young women for life as a religious filled the two years of novitiate. Hours of adoration, instructions on the vows and other aspects of religious commitment, liturgical prayer repeated in regular sequence daily, and household duties of cleaning and assisting in the kitchen made the time pass quickly. Novices learned convent ways of peeling bushels of potatoes, picking and preserving apples and pears from the orchard, making and mending clothing, and scrubbing long terrazzo hallways. They also entered into the world of quiet meditation and many oral prayers, learning how to kneel and bow in worship and how to sing Congregational hymns. It was a time for spiritual transformation, preparing Amabilis and her classmates to make profession of vows. During these years, the Great

Sister Amabilis Neumeister

Depression began to grip the country. Amabilis, fresh from the business world, was aware what this could mean to her former colleagues, and she remembered them in her prayers.

Occasionally, the novice director called upon Amabilis's expertise in office work. Still, the novitiate was a totally different world from the one she had previously known, but she took it all in "amiable" stride, living up to her new name. Profession of temporary vows on August 15, 1930, and three years later of perpetual vows, completed her formal spiritual preparation for life as a Sister of the Precious Blood.

Superiors, not sure what to do with this bright 36-year-old sister after her profession, assigned her to serve as a housekeeper at the Maria Joseph Home, an institution for the aging, adjacent to the motherhouse. This assignment required a further shifting of gears. She had to move from dealing with the intricacies of the business world to pushing brooms, clearing tables and helping residents. Her next two assignments, to Maria Stein Convent and to Kneipp Sanitarium in Rome City, Indiana, also involved domestic work. After six months in Rome City, superiors summoned her back to Salem Heights where, henceforth, she would be involved in her chosen field of business.

Treasurer General

After five years in the convent, Amabilis at last was working in a familiar milieu, doing secretarial work both for the superior of the motherhouse, Sister Victoria Drees, and for the mother superior, Mother Agreda Sperber. She quickly became familiar with the business aspects of the Congregation. With the election in 1936 of Sister Magna Lehman as mother superior, Amabilis continued serving in the administrative offices, assisting the treasurer general, Sister Macrina Kieber.

When Macrina died rather suddenly from a paralytic stroke on January 13, 1944, the General Council looked to her assistant, Amabilis, to fill the position. Sister Victoria Drees, the 80-year-old former treasurer, became her mentor. They worked together for several years, but soon Amabilis was ready to assume the role of the chief financial officer of the Sisters of the Precious Blood.

The Congregation was growing rapidly. Between 1944 and 1966, the years during which Amabilis was treasurer, the number of professed sisters grew from 671 to 831. As treasurer, she was responsible for the financial well-being of the Community, handling income and expenses, as well as donations, loans and investments. In addition, she oversaw the maintenance of all properties owned and administered by the Congregation. At the beginning of her term, besides the vast Dayton motherhouse property, the Community owned several farms, four large convents, and at least seven institutions.

There were always on-going projects set in motion by the Mother Superior and her Council or some outside force. One that took much of Amabilis's time and skill early in her tenure was a construction project that never materialized. In 1945 Cincinnati Archbishop John T. McNicholas donated to the Congregation 15 acres of land in east Dayton. On this property he asked the Congregation to build a high school to be named Brunner High School after the foundress of the Community. Complicated loans, sales, and alienations involving the Apostolic Delegate consumed Amabilis's next three years. Grave concerns about the Congregation's ability to handle construction bids of $3.6 and $3.9 million brought the problem into the election of 1948. Ultimately, Mother Nathalia Smith, who became mother superior in that election, settled the matter. On September 11, 1948, referring to the construction of the high school, Mother Nathalia wrote in her diary, "Visited with the architect, Mr. Lawrence Cotter, and canceled all further plans."

Chapter of 1948
With Mother Nathalia's election, the Congregation seemed to move into high gear, and Amabilis proved herself equal to the tasks ahead. Three months into her term, Mother Nathalia proposed building a high school structure (to be named Fatima Hall) flanking the east side of the motherhouse as an aspirancy, a high school for girls interested in entering the convent. This ambitious undertaking necessitated the borrowing of $300,000 and the selling of three Ohio convents: St.

Mary's, Dayton; Immaculate Conception, Celina; and St. Mark's, Cincinnati. The $500,000 previously allocated for Brunner High was transferred to this project. For additional funds, the Congregation mortgaged Kneipp Springs in Indiana, sold farmland in New Riegel and Marywood, Ohio, and by the end of the year, borrowed another $1,000,000.

Six months later, in order to build Lourdes Hall, a retirement and skilled nursing facility for sisters, on the west side of the motherhouse, the Community took a $500,000 lien on the motherhouse. In 1951, Regina High School in Norwood, Ohio was mortgaged to help pay for the new building. Mother Nathalia also authorized the sale of the Gruenenwald (Greenwood) buildings and farm lands, St. Mary's Convent in Phoenix, and the Marywood Pilgrim House in Thompson, Ohio along with its farmlands which the Community had owned for over 100 years.

A water shortage at Salem Heights in 1950 presented a major problem for the rapidly expanding convent. Amabilis solved this dilemma by making arrangements to tap into the Montgomery County water line. Surviving Mother Nathalia's whirlwind of activities, she met this and similar demands in her usual business-like way. Under the next administration, she would face challenges almost as great.

Chapter of 1954

The 1954 Chapter, which elected Mother Aquinas Stadtherr as mother superior, called for three new foundations: a cloister at New Reigel, Ohio; a novitiate at San Luis Rey, California; and a mission in Chile, South America. All of these required acute financial management, and Amabilis proved to be equal to the demands. An extensive renovation project at the New Riegel convent (including a lawsuit over alleged unpaid bills to the contractor) prepared the "Cradle of the Community" to house sisters desiring to lead a contemplative life. On Christmas Eve in 1955, Our Lady of the Nativity Chapel was the scene of the first Mass at the cloister. In that same year, the Community established a western novitiate at San Luis Rey, California, which already was a flourishing academy with 375 students.

No doubt the biggest challenge faced by Amabilis was the Community's first venture into mission territory. Amabilis was responsible for making all the necessary arrangements, including acquiring passports and overseas transportation. When all was complete, Mother Aquinas and four sisters—Sisters Mary John Brandewie, Ignatius Lichtle, Amalia Monnin and Geneva (Grace) Rottner—boarded a Cunard ship in New York for the long passage to Chile. They arrived on January 15, 1957. Subsequently, the Congregation established a large central house in Santiago, as well as a novitiate house in Santa Ines. Amabilis negotiated land deals and construction costs, tangled with foreign codes and procedures, and assisted Mother Aquinas in supplying the missions with everything from cornflakes to a three-ton truck. For her efforts, Amabilis later (1966) received a vacation to South America where she could witness the fruits of her labor of love for the Chilean people.

Procession before the blessing of Lourdes Hall.

While in Chile, Amabilis observed that the truck she had sent to the farm at Santa Ines had been put to good use. It supplied grains, fruits, and vegetables to the 40 to 60 sisters and candidates living at the novitiate house and at the central house in Santiago. It had also taken many children to the beach and served as a float carrying the statue of Our Lady of Mt. Carmel, patroness of Chile, on her feast day, July 16. Mother Aquinas, who served in Chile following her terms of office as mother superior, pointed out to Amabilis all that she, as treasurer, had accomplished in this mission land. Sister Marita Beumer, serving in Chile at the time, recalls that Amabilis enjoyed her trip tremendously even though she was suffering from shingles. A side trip to Valparaiso to observe the intricacies of importing merchandise fascinated her business-like mind.

Back in the States

In the meantime, in December of 1955, the Congregation purchased Melrose Manor in Ligonier, Indiana, renaming it St. Vincent's Home for the Aging. At the request of Bishop Joseph H. Albers of Lansing, Michigan, the Congregation purchased Flint Tavern, a large building with approximately 200 rooms, in downtown Flint as a home for the aging to be called Marian Hall.

Between 1954 and 1957, the Congregation renovated and made additions to the Maria Joseph Home adjacent to Salem Heights. Three new wings were added providing a chapel and additional guest rooms; a two-story auditorium and more guest rooms; and an enlarged kitchen, dining room and an infirmary with living quarters for the sisters. Cost of the project totaled $567,347. This was partially funded by the selling of farmlands, as well as by sizable donations from friends of the Congregation.

Between 1954 and 1966, the Congregation renovated the buildings, as well as the farm property, at Kneipp Springs, costing the Community $346,237. For this venture Amabilis made use of a Ford Foundation grant of $47,000, donations amounting to $30,000, and income from the sale of land to the State Highway Department.

Though care for the aging was a high priority at this time, concern for young sisters was not neglected. In September, 1960, 11 young professed sisters moved into Marycrest, a house of studies near the University of Dayton, which had been purchased for $70,000. By 1962, having outgrown Marycrest, the Community purchased a site, Maryglen, for $250,000. The Congregation was enjoying a large influx of new members at this time and could not foresee that, within a few years, these buildings would be too large.

During these years, the Congregation undertook a number of new projects. Desiring to provide opportunities for growth in spirituality among the laity, in 1960 the Congregation provided monies toward the building of a spacious retreat house in Maria Stein, Ohio. In September of 1962, Maria Stein Retreat House opened its doors for the first time. The Community also arranged for the construction of an activity center housing an Olympic-size swimming pool on the grounds of Salem Heights. The next acquisition was a cabin on Kiser Lake near New Carlisle, Ohio, where sisters could vacation.

Added to all this was Amabilis's supervision of the buildings and grounds at Salem Heights. Her responsibility included the hiring, firing, and supervising of employees for the boiler room, the lawns and gardens, the farmlands and barns, and the general maintenance of all the properties. Under her gentle but firm guidance, the employees did their work well. Amabilis managed the purchase, maintenance, and assignment of all equipment needed to run the institution and the farm. Automobiles were also under her direction, the number of which grew year by year along with the Community. Statistics from 1959-60, for instance, list 101 aspirants, 44 postulants, 51 novices, and a large number of professed sisters, active and retired, at Salem Heights.

Personal remembrances

With so much responsibility, Amabilis might well have been less than gracious when sisters came to her for small needs. Not so, says Sister Florentine Gregory, who remembers:

49

. . . how skillfully Amabilis found the train tickets on her "piled high" desk, how carefully she made travel plans and cared for banking funds. I never saw her ruffled or hurried when she explained about train time, train schedules and changes. She arranged for transportation to and from the station, as well as for taking and getting trunks and similar baggage.

This seems to have been a universal feeling about the way Amabilis treated others. Sister Agnes Christine Mullen, a co-worker with Amabilis for many years, recalls:

[Amabilis] was a great woman, holy and prayerful. She was a very talented business woman who did wonderful things for the Community, yet she was ever so humble. She had a heart of gold and was most kind to all the sisters. She was always generous with the sisters and made sure they had what they needed. She was a true friend to me.

Persons in the business world with whom Amabilis dealt regarded her with deep respect, both for her astuteness as well as her graciousness. Vincent Cashman, a teacher from Dayton who drove for the sisters while he was a student at the University of Dayton, writes the following:

Dear Sister Eleanor,
    I first met Sister Amabilis when she hired me sometime in the 40s to be a chauffeur for the Sisters of the Precious Blood. As best as I can remember, I continued in this employment until the early 50s when I graduated from the University of Dayton.
    Sister Amabilis and I always enjoyed a friendly working relationship. Her demeanor was always friendly and kind. I never saw her any other way. I could describe Sister Amabilis's personality in one word, KIND. From time to time until she went home

to Heaven, I stopped by the convent to say hello to my good friend.

Sincerely yours,
Vincent Cashman

Sister Rose Habig, a classmate of Amabilis, recalls accompanying her for an appointment with a banker. When he shook hands with Amabilis, he called her "Ama-bliss"! One can imagine her short, somewhat portly frame walking away, with her face blushing. Amabilis was a lady with a business-like appearance on the outside and a good sincere heart on the inside.

Chapter of 1966

New life burst forth in the Congregation with the Chapter of 1966. Amabilis was now 72, and it was time for her to make way for another generation of leadership. The winds of Vatican II were blowing strong, and technological advances were changing the way business was done. Her mode of operation had been a traditional one, but one in which the Community had fared well. However, the time for change had come.

For the previous 34 years, Amabilis had directed the financial transactions of the Congregation. It is amazing that when the administration of Sister Rosella Hess took the reins of leadership in 1966, after 18 years of extensive building and expansion, there was no Congregational debt. Amabilis's methods of directing the finances of the Community seemed almost miraculous. However, the devotion, energy and power built up through those years could not psychologically dissipate overnight. That spelled trouble for the incoming administration and especially for the new treasurer, Sister Dorothy Kammerer. After Dorothy assumed the position, Amabilis continued making major financial decisions without consulting anyone. She was even reluctant to give up her treasurer's office.

Things came to a head one day when Dorothy left the treasurer's office for a short time. Upon her return, Amabilis told her that the sisters from Chile had called, and since they needed money immediately, she had written a check for $20,000! A session with the newly elected superior was necessary to iron things out. Sister Rosella gently told Amabilis that she was no longer treasurer. It was difficult for Amabilis to leave the work she had obviously found both challenging and stimulating. But the Congregation had spoken, and reluctantly but obediently, she removed her things from the office.

Despite the problems created for her in pursuing her responsibilities, Dorothy had this to say of her predecessor:

> [Amabilis] was really a nice soul with a wealth of information at her fingertips. Important information was easily accessible as she kept that type of material in cardboard boxes under her desk. And look at all the rare advice she gave us while looking for a roadmap, or an envelope that had car keys in it, or an envelope containing money we were to use for food on the way to our mission in case we became hungry. . . . Human nature occasionally knocks on the door of the human heart saying, "I am still here."

Life draws to a close

After 1966, Amabilis worked in the post office at Salem Heights until January of 1970. At that time she was diagnosed with metastic odenocarcinoma of the breast. She died on November 15 that same year. The *Catholic Telegraph* of November 20, 1970 lauded her as "one who played a key role in the development and financial soundness of the facilities and operations of the Community."

The *CPPS Dialog* noted that "business men in Dayton expressed their great respect for her and acknowledged her as a woman of universal business ability with keen foresight in business." In the same issue, Mother Aquinas, speaking of the years she had served with her, said: "Sister Amabilis was a humble, prayerful religious Sister; [she] never tried to make a show of herself, never sought popularity, always tried to stay in the background."

Operating out of a tiny, rather chaotic office, Amabilis amazingly brought order and stability to a rapidly growing Congregation. Devoted to her work and possessing a keen mind for business, she was an example of a gifted person bearing great responsibilities with humility and grace.

Healing Hands

*Stories of Sisters
Who Served in the Nursing Ministry*

By Helen Weber CPPS

Early years

Uttering a soft moan, the elderly sister tossed restlessly in her bed. A white-clothed nun quietly approached her, and with gentle words soothed her sweaty brow with a cool cloth. Comforted, the patient drifted into a welcome sleep. The end of her journey would be soon, and the presence of a kind and loving sister-nurse would ease her passing.

As loving members of a family, the Sisters of the Precious Blood have always provided care for their own. Reflecting the custom of the Community since its beginning, the 1946 Constitution of the Congregation (Art. 187, p. 74) directed that "One or more sisters who excel in charity and ability shall be appointed to take care of the sick." Although never intending nursing to be a primary ministry, from the earliest days superiors of the Congregation have regarded it as their sacred duty to be attentive to the sick and elderly and to assign compassionate sisters to care for them.

Until the development of small teaching communities living in parish houses, the sisters lived in large convents. Often, special rooms were set aside as an infirmary, and one or more sisters acted as infirmarians, using medical practices current at the time.

Mother Ludovica Scharf, the first elected mother superior after the separation from the men's Community in 1887, was deeply concerned about the physical needs of the sisters. She encouraged sister-cooks to serve more nourishing meals, and sister-infirmarians to be especially kind to the sick. In 1895, Mother Ludovica, accompanied by Sister Margaret Schlachter, the mistress of novices, traveled to Europe to recruit candidates for the Congregation at the filial house in Schellenberg, Liechtenstein. While there, she heard about a hydrotherapy program promoted by a priest-physician, Reverend Doctor Sebastian Kneipp (1821-1897).

After discussing with her companion the possible value of the program for the Congregation, Mother Ludovica decided that Margaret should remain in Europe to study hydrotherapy so that she could bring it to America for the benefit of the sisters. Margaret participated in the several-month course at Woerishofen, Bavaria under the founder, Father Kneipp. By doing so, she became the first sister in the Community to receive specialized training in health care. During her stay in Europe, she learned both the theory and the practices connected with the hydrotherapeutic system known as Kneipp therapy.

Kneipp therapy

Since Father Kneipp was very poor when he was young, he worked as a herdsboy and a bricklayer. A combination of hard work and poor nutrition left him severely weakened and almost prevented him from fulfilling his desire to become a priest. In the seminary, he became gravely ill with tuberculosis, forcing him to leave his studies. While working to support himself, he spent his free time in the local library where he came upon a booklet entitled "Instructions on the Virtue and Efficiency of Fresh Water" by Johann Sigmund Hahn.

With delight, he read and re-read the booklet and began a personal regimen that included bathing in the icy Danube even in wintertime. The result was the restoration of his health, enabling him to return to the seminary. So convinced was he of the efficacy of hydrotherapy that he began to employ its practices systematically, not only on himself, but on his classmates as well.

Several years after ordination, Sebastian became pastor of Woerishofen. In this small village, he acquired knowledge of agriculture and the curative powers of fresh air, sunlight and natural foods. Combining this information with the principles of hydrotherapy, he designed a holistic therapeutic program, similar in many ways to some that are popular today. His program caught on, and his village became a center for training in the methods he had designed. At this center, Margaret Schlachter studied all aspects of Kneipp therapy: water treatments, diet control, the curative value of fresh air and sunshine, and the effects on bodily functions of teas made from certain plants.

Sister Margaret Schlachter (1855-1910)

Margaret was born in 1855 in Cleveland, Ohio to immigrant parents who had come to America between 1850 and 1855. Her older siblings had been born in Baden, Germany. She joined the Sisters of the Precious Blood at Maria Stein, Ohio on June 8, 1879 when she was 24 years old. Two aunts and three of Margaret's older sisters—Crispina, Gottlieba, and Felicitas—preceded her in the Community. Her brother, Godfrey, became a missionary priest.

Margaret took the Oath of Allegiance in the Congregation in 1884, and professed vows in 1885. Already in 1887, she became director of novices at age 32. As previously mentioned, in 1895 she studied Kneipp therapy under Father Sebastian Kneipp. Returning to Maria Stein, she employed its techniques and practices in the care of the sisters. She was enthusiastic about the therapy, and the sisters enjoyed its full benefits. *Not With Silver or Gold,* the Community history, says that "Kneipping became quite the vogue for the sisters. . . ." (p. 284).

Sister Margaret Schlachter

Kneipp Springs

Margaret's life took another turn in 1899 when she was elected secretary on the General Council during Mother Emma Nunlist's first term. A sanitarium near Rome City, Indiana constructed and managed by Doctor William Geiermann, an enthusiastic hydrotherapist, had fallen upon hard times. Mother Emma had been a patient there and was impressed both by the beauty of the place and the value of the treatment she received. Dr. Geiermann, desiring that a religious community continue his work, approached Mother Emma about purchasing the place. His request fascinated her. With two council members, Mother Ludovica and Margaret, she visited the institution, and in 1901 the Congregation became the new owner of Kneipp Sanitarium.

Although Margaret was a member of the General Council, she accepted the appointment as the first administrator and superior of Kneipp Sanitarium. To these positions, she brought leadership, knowledge and enthusiasm for hydrotherapy. She shared her knowledge and skills with sisters appointed to provide therapy to guests. The first two sisters Margaret trained in hydrotherapy were Sister Bonavita Oliger who served at the Sanitarium from 1901 until 1951 and Sister Nuntia Kreilinger who performed the therapy treatments from 1903 to 1958. Margaret's convictions about the value of the therapy, together with her management skills, turned the sanitarium into a thriving institution. Kneipp Springs, the name adopted in 1939, was the first major effort in public health care by the Sisters of the Precious Blood.

Margaret remained at Kneipp Sanitarium until her death in 1910. During these years, she also continued to be active in various Congregational activities. She returned to Europe several times to recruit candidates for the Community. She also accompanied Mother Emma to the beatification of Gaspar del Bufalo in Rome in December, 1904. The visit to the Eternal City and the ceremony honoring the founder of the Precious Blood Society were the high points of Margaret's life.

The Congregation acquired Kneipp Sanitarium in 1901.

Margaret' s death

Margaret was only 55 years old when she died on March 27, 1910 at St. Joseph's Hospital in Fort Wayne, Indiana. In her relatively short life, she endeared herself not only to members of her Community but also to everyone who knew her. Describing her death, *Not With Silver or Gold* says:

> . . . After a serious operation a year earlier, [Margaret] was in such a critical condition that the doctor declared her case hopeless unless she were operated on again. Holy Thursday eve found her still active as superior of Kneipp Sanitarium. While busy overseeing the erection of a beautiful crucifixion group . . . she was summoned to meet her missionary brother, Father Godfrey Schlachter, who appeared unusually perturbed. He had come to urge her to submit to the operation, which three days later proved fatal.
>
> Sister Margaret is remembered . . . as a person of quiet dignity and calm determination. . . . During her eight years' superiorship at the sanitarium she won the esteem of doctors, patients, and all who came in contact with her. Her presence of mind in an

emergency and her utter reliability at all times especially fitted her for her position. Her passing removed one of the foundation stones of the community (p. 312).

Margaret's death stunned the community in Rome City. She had been the enthusiastic leader and the heart of the institution for the entire nine years of its existence as a ministry of the Congregation. She had passed on her firsthand knowledge of Kneipp therapy and shared her unique spirit with both staff and guests. She would be sorely missed. The untimely death of its vibrant leader threatened the still young institution.

Sister Ottilia Heckman was Margaret's immediate successor as administrator and superior. A year later, in 1911, these duties fell to Sister Agreda Sperber, who had served as treasurer of the Sanitarium since its beginning in 1901. Agreda, who continued as administrator and superior even though she was elected treasurer of the Congregation in 1911, proved to be the ideal choice. Mastering all facets of management, she brought to the administration a keen understanding of its financial situation. She held both positions until 1920 when she moved to the motherhouse at Maria Stein.

Later years

Kneipp Sanitarium flourished under Agreda's leadership. The number of guests increased and, as a result, many more sisters were needed as nurses. The Congregation constructed additional buildings and facilities, even an operating room that was used until local hospitals could provide this service. The institution continued to carry out its original purpose of offering hydrotherapy.

Sisters assigned as nurses in Rome City in the early years included Sisters Milburgis Lichtenauer, Solome Ruen, Coelina Schick, and Elvira Derby. Although none of them received the specialized training in hydrotherapy that Margaret had, they learned on the job and became proficient at giving the treatments. Because of the great need for more sister-nurses, superiors carefully observed novices helping in the Maria Stein infirmary to determine which ones had the necessary personal qualifications and abilities to become nurses.

In addition to being mentored by others, some of the nurses received other opportunities to advance their skills. Sisters Elvira Derby and Rosanna Russell took a course at Rose College of Chiropractic Medicine in Fort Wayne, Indiana. They practiced their new skills in the care of young sisters at Maria Stein. Elvira, who had been at the Sanitarium since 1918, returned there and continued giving the hydrotherapy treatments until 1975 when she retired.

Along with the rest of the nation during the Great Depression beginning in 1929, Kneipp Sanitarium endured hard times, though it continued to serve a limited number of clients. The story of Sister Ludgeria Bellinghausen in Volume II of this series describes the financial recovery of the institution after the Depression. Later in this volume, the story of Sister Mercedes Eberle, the "tea sister," reveals another facet of the work there.

Both in this country and abroad, Kneipp Springs received attention as a unique kind of health care institution. Word of mouth brought clients from many parts of the United States, primarily the Midwest. A German newspaper carried an article which said in part:

America is the land of great opportunities. What appeared impossible in the birth place of Monsignor Kneipp became a reality in the USA in a place called KNEIPP SPRINGS. Another thing made possible by the Americans is this, this place is only 60 kilometers from ROME CITY. Both Kneipp Springs and Rome City are in the State of Indiana, southeast of Lake Michigan. The Kneipp Metropolis in Woerishofen was recently visited by two Sisters of the Precious Blood . . . Sister Mary Josina [Kuhn], Superior and Sister [Margaret] Mary Flinn, a nurse. They came to see for themselves the direction and operation of the Kneipp Cure of Sebastian Kneipp.

In addition to Margaret Schlacter and others mentioned above, three sisters who contributed to the work at the Sanitarium deserve mention: Sisters Coelina Schick, Mercedes Eberle, and Mary Joseph Nufer.

Sister Coelina Schick (1889-1969)

Born in Langenschemmern, Germany, Mary Schick came to America in 1910, at the age of 21, to enter the Sisters of the Precious Blood. Leaving behind three sisters and two brothers, she traveled with Sister Regula Dann, the novice mistress, and Sister Oswalda Hoege who had come to Europe to recruit new members for the Congregation.

At investiture Mary received the name, Sister Mary Coelina. Her nursing career began almost immediately. Within a year, she was at Kneipp Sanitarium learning hydrotherapy. She served there for the next 13 years, where, in

Sister Coelina Schick

addition to giving the treatments, she became the personal nurse of the administrator, Sister Agreda Sperber, who was a diabetic. When Agreda was elected mother superior in 1924, Coelina joined her at the motherhouse where they both remained for 12 years.

As infirmarian at Salem Heights, Coelina was the primary caregiver for sisters, novices and postulants. In this role she served with dedication and gentle concern, dispensing common sense along with medical advice. She continued to monitor Mother Agreda's health. Their relationship was the basis for what was possibly the greatest adventure of her life—a trip to Europe!

In 1933, as part of the Congregation's centenary celebration, Mother Agreda, accompanied by Sisters Adelaide Walz and Coelina, went to Europe to bring the body of Maria Anna Brunner, the foundress of the Congregation, to America. They were present for the exhumation and identification of Mother Brunner's body—a moving experience for them all.

After Mother Agreda completed 12 years as mother superior, she returned to Kneipp Sanitarium. Coelina accompanied her and continued to act as her nurse until Mother Agreda's death in 1938. The following year, Coelina went to St. Mary's Seminary in Cincinnati for four years, followed by a four-year stint of nursing at Maria Joseph Home. In 1947, she returned to Kneipp Springs and spent another seven years there, bringing to a total of 23 the number of years she spent in Rome City. After serving for two years in the host department at Salem Heights, she retired to Lourdes Hall, the health care facility for the sisters, where she helped wherever she could until her death in 1969 of multiple health problems.

Sister Mercedes Eberle (1890-1984)

Through the mist of an early summer morning, a figure in black hustles forward, intent upon her mission. Her bird-like movements are quick and somewhat jerky, but unhesitant in their quest. The tall slender nun hurries through the thick grass into a patch of weeds and wild plants. Stopping momentarily, she shoos a rabbit away from its breakfast of green herbs. Bending over, she snips the flowers from several plants, shakes off the dew, and puts them into the basket on her arm.

Early morning is the best time to pick the flowers to assure their full medicinal strength. Since she has been working in this herb garden for over 30 years, she knows the exact location of every plant and can do her work quickly. Never late for prayer, she hurries toward chapel as the morning haze begins to rise. Sister Mercedes Eberle, the "tea sister," begins another day's work at Kneipp Sanitarium. When she was assigned to the Sanitarium in 1910, the Congregation had owned and operated it for only nine years.

Background

Eulalia Eberle was born in 1890 in Altschweier, Baden, Germany, the fourth child of Lorenz and Caecilia Huber Eberle. When Eulalia was 16 years old, Sister Felicitas Schlachter, the sister of Margaret Schlachter, and her companion, Sister Anselma Rufle, came to her village to recruit young women for the Sisters of the Precious Blood. Many years later, Eulalia wrote about this in her autobiography:

> I made up my mind to go to the convent, and at that time the Sisters used to come to Germany to pick up girls who wanted to join the Sisters of the Precious Blood. I was acquainted with Sister Regis Kirschner who was our neighbor. She had a niece [Sister Marina Jost] and we were close and we went to school together. . . . We made up our minds, we two, that we wanted to go to America, to the Sisters of the Precious Blood. In 1906 . . . Sister Felicitas and Sister Anselma came to pick up the girls, and we said we want to go along, and of course, our parents let us go. . . . We reached Maria Stein on September 24, 1906.

Later in the same document, Mercedes speaks highly of her novice mistress, Sister Regula Dann, and of the saintly Father Henry Drees. Her memories include glowing words of praise for Mother Ludovica who welcomed the 24 young women from Germany when they arrived at Maria Stein. The warm reception by the sisters eased the pangs of homesickness for this group so far from their native land.

During the summers when the sister-teachers returned to Maria Stein from their missions, there was not enough room for both sisters and novices. To solve this problem, the novices spent part of each summer at various mission houses. While she was a novice, Eulalia, now Sister Mercedes, helped with the cooking in Minster, Ohio. In her autobiography, she shared an amusing experience from this time:

> *During my novitiate I was sent to Minster Convent for a few months where I helped Sister Tertulla [Gerber] in the kitchen. One time Rev. Mother Josephine came there on visitation, and Sister Superior sent me in to see Rev. Mother. My visit must not have been very exciting because good Mother fell asleep. I thought I couldn't walk out while she was sleeping. So finally she woke up and said, "Oh, my child, are you still here?" I answered, "Yes." She said a few more words and then said, "You go and be a good child."*

First mission

After profession of first vows on April 6, 1910, Mercedes went to Kneipp Sanitarium to assist in nursing under the direction of Sister Bonavita Oliger. Mercedes later wrote, *I didn't know anything about nursing at all. I had to learn everything the hard way.* She credits Bonavita and Sister Nuntia Grueulinger for initiating her into nursing and for teaching her sensitive and compassionate care of patients. She describes at length the treatments given by the sisters at the Sanitarium. Because she believed these treatments relaxed and renewed the patients, she experienced great satisfaction in administering them.

While assisting Nuntia, Mercedes began the work for which she is well known—tending the herb garden and making the herbal teas that were a vital part of Kneipp therapy. After the death of Sister Egbertha Bloedt who had been in charge of the herb garden, Nuntia took on her responsibilities and gradually taught all she knew to Mercedes. When Nuntia began teaching her, Mercedes said she *didn't know a herb from a weed.* She shared a memory from this experience:

> *I went out with Sister Nuntia and we worked in the herb garden. . . . She said "I have to do some work inside, you do this and then I'll come back." After a while she came out and there was a real nice stalk there. I thought to myself, " I don't know what this is. It must be a herb, I better let it stand." When she came I said "What's that?" She said that it was a thistle. So after that, I knew a thistle. That is how I learned the herbs.*

The "tea lady"

After a short time, Nuntia suggested to Agreda, the administrator, that Mercedes take over the garden and the making of the teas. Although Mercedes continued to give the treatments, preparation of the teas increasingly occupied more of her time. Since each plant required special care, the herb garden needed constant attention. It was necessary to harvest each plant at the proper time to procure the maximum amount of curative value from it. Though it took her years to master all she needed to know, Mercedes eventually became an expert "tea lady."

Mercedes guarded her herb garden with great care. Neither the guests nor the hired men had access to it. Even the

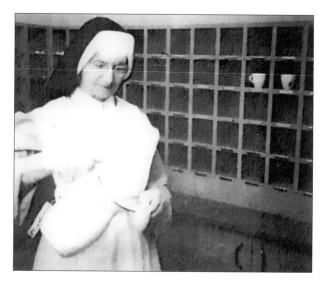

Mercedes prepared medicinal teas for guests at Kneipp Springs.

sisters knew better than to stray into it. Sister Margaret (De Porres) Morris recalls that, when she arrived as sacristan at Kneipp Springs, Mercedes immediately informed her that the flowers blooming in the herb garden were not to be used in the chapel!

The therapy at the Sanitarium made use of the curative powers of nature. Besides producing flowers or leaves with which to make the various kinds of teas, the herb garden also yielded plants for herb treatment baths. After harvesting and drying the various flowers and leaves to make the teas, the stalks were dried and stored in the attic. Later, they were packed into bags and immersed in boiling water to be used for wrapping or soaking—treatments for the relief of the pains of arthritis, rheumatism and similar maladies.

Mercedes mixed the ingredients for the teas with great precision. For example: a recipe for a tea prescribed to relieve pain included: four parts chamomile, five parts elder blossoms, four parts balm leaves, three parts anise, three parts fennel and three parts caraway. Similar recipes existed for sedative tea, kidney tea, liver or gall stone tea, stomach tea, laxative tea, blood purifying tea, and tea for colds.

After the resident physician prescribed the appropriate tea for a patient, Mercedes poured the assigned tea into a small cup. She then placed it in the tea room in a cubbyhole marked with the patient's name. As part of the treatment, all guests received a "supper tea" that the sister-cooks made in huge quantities. This tea was a relaxing herbal tea containing strawberry leaves, violet leaves and blossoms, linden blossoms and wood root. A complete listing of the teas and their ingredients is available at the Heritage Museum in Maria Stein, Ohio.

Mercedes's later years

Mercedes was a familiar and much-loved fixture at the Springs where she ministered for 62 years. Sisters and guests recall her wide-ranging stories, her dry and subtle sense of humor, and the wisdom she brought to all situations. Twice she enjoyed the privilege of visiting her home country of

Germany. In 1965, after 50 years in America, she traveled with Sister Mauritia Mueller, via the Queen Mary, to see her relatives. She described the reunion:

> It was the year of my golden jubilee . . . a great home-coming. I was in the company of Sister Mauritia Mueller from my neighboring village, Sister Expedita [Strittmatter] and Sister Johanna [Adelgoss]. . . . When they met us at the station . . . Sister Mauritia's people were there, her sisters and, oh, my people! They brought us flowers—my brother and my sister. My sister from the convent came home for 2 or 3 weeks, she had permission to come home when I came home. She was at the station and I had never met her before [as an adult]. . . . When I came home to my parent's home, they had the house decorated . . . and a big dinner for me. My nephews were there. . . . They had grape wine . . . the best wine that grows around there. . . . Afterward I said to my brother, "That's strong," he said, "That's all right, you only get that once when you come home after 50 years."

Mercedes continued her grueling schedule of taking care of the herb garden, making the teas and giving treatments until 1970 when she fell and broke her hip. She was then 80 years old. Of this period she says: *After the fall I couldn't nurse anymore. I couldn't carry a tray, and I couldn't give the treatments anymore. I didn't feel like I shouldn't, I just couldn't. I couldn't do my work right any more; I couldn't go into the tea garden. . . .*

So, after 62 years Mercedes asked her superiors to relieve her of her duties and allow her to go to Emma Hall, the infirmary for the sisters in Dayton, Ohio. She dealt with this change in her life in a very matter-of-fact way, except to make the point that, before she left Kneipp Springs, someone else must be ready to take over the herb garden. In 1976 when she was 86 years old, she apparently felt well enough to visit Germany once again, this time by air.

In Emma Hall, Mercedes spent her time knitting and crocheting baby booties, caps, and afghans for the Diversional Activities Center. In 1981 she celebrated 75 years in the

Mercedes spent her last days in Lourdes Hall

Congregation. Gradually, her health deteriorated, and she suffered a great deal. She had always been a hard worker, so it was very difficult for her to feel useless, even at 94. She could no longer pray as she wished or be fully present to her sisters. Mercedes died on December 29, 1984 in the 79th year of her religious life.

Sister Mary Joseph Nufer (1905-1999)

Mary Elizabeth Nufer was born into a family of four boys and four girls in Winamac, Indiana on April 27, 1905. Her parents were Andrew and Josephine Nufer. She learned about the Sisters of the Precious Blood through her cousin and godmother, Sister Rosetta Weber, who together with Mother Agreda Sperber, had entered the Congregation from Winamac previously. Rosetta's story appears in Volume I of this series. Mary Elizabeth entered the Community in Dayton, Ohio in 1927 at age 22.

After her first profession in 1930, Sister Mary Joseph, the name Mary Elizabeth received at investiture, taught for four years in Ohio schools. In the summer of 1933, Mother Agreda asked her if she would be interested in becoming a registered nurse. Mary Joseph responded affirmatively and began to prepare for the intense education involved in becoming a nurse. She enrolled in Our Lady Help of Christians School of

Nursing at St. Mary's Hospital in Cincinnati in 1933. Three years later, Mary Joseph was officially a registered nurse, the fourth Precious Blood sister to become one.

With the encouragement of Mother Agreda, Mary Joseph began her 18-year tenure of service at Kneipp Springs. During the Chapter of 1954, Mary Joseph was elected first assistant to Mother Aquinas Stadtherr and served in this capacity for 12 years. During these years, she traveled extensively, visiting the Community's missions in the United States and Chile. She also accompanied Sister Mary Alice (Mary Paul) Wurm, who suffered from multiple sclerosis, on a pilgrimage to Lourdes, France in 1960. Following her terms of office, Mary Joseph served as Director of Nursing for the seriously ill and aged sisters at the motherhouse. In 1971, after an absence of 17 years, Mary Joseph returned to Rome City as Director of Nursing.

As a native Hoosier and veteran of 17 years at the Springs, she was happy to return to Indiana and to Kneipp Springs. She worked there until her retirement in 1975 when she took up residence at Salem Heights. Of her return to

Sister Mary Joseph Nufer

Dayton, she said, *Within a short time . . . I found myself to be the "Foot Nurse"—bringing relief to many sisters' painful, aching feet.* She also found time to enjoy hobbies and is especially remembered for her tube or liquid embroidery.

In 1994 Mary Joseph moved from Salem Heights to Emma Hall, the infirmary for the sisters in the Maria Joseph Living Care Center. There she maintained her prayerful spirit and offered up her physical suffering for the needs of others. She died peacefully on November 28, 1999. She was 94 years of age, having served the Congregation for 72 years.

Closing the Springs

By the early 1970s, after a period during which the Springs again flourished, the institution began to experience hard times. Many factors brought this about: a changing society, increasing state regulation, a rising economy, and fewer religious personnel professionally trained for services in a modern health spa. The Congregation faced this reality squarely and discerned that the time had come to discontinue its services at Kneipp Springs.

During the 75 years that the Sisters of the Precious Blood owned and operated the Springs, hundreds of sisters served there as nurses, housekeepers, cooks, bookkeepers and office

Mary Joseph ministered at Kneipp Springs for a total of 21 years.

personnel. An article in the *CPPS Dialog* (January, 1977) by
Sister Berenice Janszen, Northern Region Councilor, describes
the closing of the institution:

> And so it was that on November 18, 1976, just
> twenty-two days short of seventy-five years of serv-
> ice, the Congregation, under the leadership of Sister
> Charmaine Grilliot, sold the Springs to Mr. Theodore
> Leinsinger from Ft. Wayne, Indiana. A life circle of
> love, prayer, and service was closed with gratitude to
> God for His innumerable blessings through the
> years, with gratitude to the hundreds of unsung
> heroines who through the years dedicated their
> religious lives to God's work there, and with grati-
> tude to the thousands of people who came to the
> Springs to share God's goodness. . . .

Other nursing ventures

Kneipp Sanitarium was the Congregation's only
health care facility for adult laity from 1901 to 1930 when the
Maria Joseph Home opened in Dayton, Ohio. During that
period, sister nurses were also active as infirmarians in the
large convents and in the orphanages. When the Salem
Heights motherhouse in Dayton reached its completion in
1923, Sisters Milburgis and Coelina served as nurses there.
Since they came from the Sanitarium, they used hydrotherapy
and other natural medicines to treat the sisters.

At various times in the history of the Congregation, sisters provided health care to the needy in their homes. In 1936
Sister Adelaide Waltz, reflecting on the Congregation's first
100 years, wrote in *The Voice of Praise:*

> In earlier days, custom urged the Sisters to visit
> the sick-poor in their homes. How often an afflicted
> mother, lying helpless in the last stages of some
> dreadful disease, was solaced by the regular
> appearance of a Sister of the Precious Blood who

brought not only comfort but provisions as well. Times of stress, as in the cholera and influenza epidemics, found our Sisters ready volunteers (Vol. 2, Ch. XI, p. 6).

During the influenza epidemic in 1918, sisters at Maria Stein gave assistance to families in desperate need. Heedless of the possibility of catching the dreaded disease themselves, many sisters volunteered for this ministry. An unsigned account of sisters responding as good neighbors appears in the Archives of the Congregation:

In the fall of 1918 the flu epidemic struck families in Mercer County and people were dying right and left. The Link family at St. Peter's, Ohio—like other families at St. Anthony's, Philothea, St. Joseph's, Coldwater, etc., turned to the Sisters at Maria Stein Convent for help. Sr. Adelbertha Fischer volunteered to go into the Link home and take care of Mr. & Mrs. Link and their four children. An aunt came in by day to take care of the family, and Sister took care of them during the night. Mr. Link was delirious with a high fever for 3 weeks, and lost 60 pounds. Sister bathed him frequently with cold water, prayed over him and sprinkled him with holy water, Mrs. Link and the three older children were not too sick. Julie [later Sister Edigna] was just a baby, and when Sister Adelbertha took care of her, she prayed that some day little Julie would become a sister and take her place. . . .

Sister Adelbertha remained at the Link home for eight weeks. She didn't leave until Mr. Link was well and gained back a little weight and strength. . . . Sister Julie Link [d. 1995] remembers accompanying her mother and dad to the funeral of Sr. Adelbertha who died at Dayton on October 1, 1926. Sister Julie remembers kneeling at Sister's grave . . . with her mother and dad.

Education of nurses

Over the years, the Congregation recognized the need to educate additional sisters as nurses. In 1931, Mother Agreda assigned two sisters—Sisters Rolendis Pool and Germaine Butz—to enter the nursing program at Our Lady Help of Christians School of Nursing operated by the Franciscan Sisters of Hartwell in Cincinnati, Ohio. In order to become registered nurses, they completed the three-year course and passed the State Board Examination in Columbus, Ohio. They were the first sisters in the Community to achieve this goal. Because both were sent to Rome City, they also met all the qualifications for licensing in the state of Indiana.

Within the next two years, Sisters Agatha Koesters and Mary Joseph Nufer also entered the program. Mother Agreda's long experience at Kneipp Sanitarium prompted her to assure professional training for the sister-nurses, and her successors followed her lead. During Mother Magna Lehman's term (1936–1948), Sister Mildred (Venard) Westendorf and Sister Mary Raymond Chappie graduated as registered nurses from Good Samaritan Hospital in Dayton. Sisters Virginia (Claudine) Hebbeler, Nivard Williams, and Margaret Mary (Innocent) Imes earned R.N.s while Mother Nathalia was in office (1948-1954). Also under Mother Nathalia, Sisters Mary Cleophas Schumacher and Ann Ella Kiacz became licensed practical nurses.

Since Mother Nathalia's time in office, sisters desiring ministry in the health care profession have had the opportunity to receive professional training. Some sisters, however, continued to provide generous and sensitive care for many years without any special training. In this group were Sister Mauritia Mueller who was infirmarian at Maria Stein for almost 40 years and Sister Elvira Derby who, except for the year at the Chiropractic School, worked at Kneipp Springs from 1918 through 1975.

Serving the elderly

Beginning in the 1920s, the Congregation began to respond to the growing need for improved care of elderly persons. During the next three decades, it opened and operated three homes for aging persons in Ohio and Indiana.

Maria Joseph Home for the Aged

As early as 1921, a group of women in Dayton conceived a plan for building a facility to accommodate elderly persons who desired to spend their declining years in a religious environment. They pledged to cooperate with the Sisters of the Precious Blood in raising funds. At that time, however, the Congregation was deeply involved in the construction of the new motherhouse in Dayton. Nevertheless, the concept was agreed upon, and in a few years, the construction of the Maria Joseph Home for the Aged began.

Maria Joseph Home opened for occupancy September 1, 1930 with two of the five proposed wings completed. Sister Philippine Foltz was its first director. This marked the beginning of a new and important ministry in the Congregation—care of the elderly. In 1938, rooms in the Home were set aside for sick residents, and Sister Rolendis Pool became the first registered nurse to serve there. *More Than the Doing*, by Sisters Janet Davis Richardson CSJP and Canice Werner CPPS, recounts the significance of the Maria Joseph Home at that time:

> It is neither redundant nor self-serving to recall that in an era when institutional care for the elderly was in its budding stages, the Sisters of the Precious Blood played an innovative role. The Church gained both experience and service from a facility such as Maria Joseph Home, somewhat new on the national scene at this time. . . (p. 138).

In 1960 the Maria Joseph Home expanded with the completion of the original design, with five wings radiating from a center rotunda (see story of Sister Grace Pratt earlier in this volume for details). The excellent reputation of the institution ensured full capacity, but the emerging need for a variety of care in residences for the aging precipitated several moves that affected both the Congregation and its nursing ministry.

As the number of novices drastically declined in the late 70s, Salem Heights had a considerable amount of under-utilized space. This fact, coupled with the growing need for varied levels of care for the aging, led Congregational leadership to initiate the remodeling of the entire Salem Heights complex into independent living apartments, assisted living units and rooms for skilled nursing care.

Beginning in 1969, sick and infirm sisters were moved from Lourdes Hall to the third floor of the main building. This unit became known as Emma Hall in memory of Mother Emma Nunlist who had pioneered the relocation of the motherhouse from Maria Stein to Dayton in 1923. This move was followed by the renovation of Lourdes Hall to accommodate residents of the Maria Joseph Home needing skilled care.

In 1975 the remodeling of the rest of the motherhouse began. By 1979, the remaining residents of Maria Joseph moved into the renovated building. Because of the positive name recognition of the Maria Joseph Home, the new entity was called the Maria Joseph Living Care Center. The sisters who had been residing in the motherhouse moved to the old Maria Joseph Home which became the new Salem Heights motherhouse. The Living Care Center continued under the management of the Congregation until 1985 when it was sold to Samaritan Health Resources, Inc., a Catholic nursing care corporation.

St. Vincent's Home

Shortly after her election in 1952, Mother Aquinas Stadtherr responded to the need for a home for the aged in northern Indiana. The Congregation purchased Melrose Manor, a three-story mansion with 16 rooms, situated on 7.8 acres of land in Ligonier, Indiana. In order to meet state health codes, the building needed repair and renovation. Workmen from Ligonier, Kneipp Springs and Dayton, as well as a contingent of Precious Blood sisters, pitched in to help. The active cooperation of Catholic organizations inspired the general public to lend a hand. By June 1, 1956, St. Vincent's Home for the Aged was ready for occupancy.

Sisters Feliciana Pffirmann and Christiana (Teresa) Smyth administered the Home for a brief time until Sister Agatha Koesters became administrator and nurse on November 3, 1958. The reputation of the nursing care, meals, and general excellence of St. Vincent's spread quickly. As a result, it was soon necessary for the Home to develop a waiting list.

As early as 1963, there was discussion of new construction. Mother Aquinas approached Bishop Leo Pursley of Fort Wayne concerning a possible site. Within a year, initial plans were drawn for two wings, the first phase of a new structure. The Community, however, began to experience a decrease in membership and was no longer able to provide administrators and staff. Since no options for replacements were available, the Congregation dropped plans for further development. Current residents were placed in other nursing homes, and the doors to St. Vincent's closed on August 19, 1967.

Sisters Leonilla Frietch, Agatha Koesters, BerniceKruezek
and Miriam Disselkamp pose in front of St. Vincent's.

Sister Agatha Koesters (1906-1994)

Bertha Koesters was born May 22, 1906 on the family farm near Carthagena, Ohio to Bernard and Catherine Link Koesters. She was the fifth child in a family of nine, having six brothers and two sisters. Her role as middle child in a large family taught her to be self sufficient, resilient and able to relate well with others—characteristics she exhibited throughout her life.

After she completed her basic education, she followed the custom of many young women in rural areas by assisting families with infants or elderly parents. While Bertha was still a teenager, her older sister, Christina, who became Sister Mary Justina, entered the Sisters of the Precious Blood at Maria Stein, Ohio.

In 1927, at the age of 21, Bertha also entered the Congregation. During her novitiate she completed her high school education. After profession of vows, Sister Agatha, as she was known in religion, was assigned to teach in the primary grades. She quickly discovered that teaching was not a

Sister Agatha Koesters

good fit for her. Mother Agreda, who was familiar with the nursing needs of the Congregation due to her many years at Kneipp Sanitarium, sent Agatha to begin nursing school in 1932. She became a registered nurse in 1935.

Agatha's first duty as a nurse was to care for sick and infirm sisters at Salem Heights. After a short while, she became head nurse and remained in that position until 1949. After a stint of nine years as night supervisor, and later, as head nurse at Kneipp Springs, she became administrator at St. Vincent's.

Under Agatha's leadership, St. Vincent's Home flourished. The sisters' presence did much to overcome anti-Catholic sentiment in that part of Indiana. Agatha's name was almost synonymous with St. Vincent's. She arrived there shortly after it opened and remained until it closed. She was widely recognized as a compassionate and competent nurse and administrator. She became known for her decisive manner and her ability to communicate with everyone. Her twinkling blue eyes and her deep chuckle eased many a difficult situation.

Agatha returned to Salem Heights where she served for two years before beginning a very active retirement. In 1974, she went to Russell's Point, Ohio where she worked with senior citizens in St. Mary's Parish. Later, she lived in the Ottoville convent where she soon became a favorite of the village inhabitants. Sister Barbara Jean Backs, who lived with Agatha in Ottoville, recalls:

> During her stay in Ottoville, one of Agatha's duties was to walk to the post office each day for the mail. As in many small towns, the post office was a meeting place for retired folks. Many times their language was not something she could approve of. So, with the usual twinkle in her eye, she'd ask, *You guys saying a new kind of rosary?* They would laugh, but after a while, they cleaned up their language when they saw Agatha approaching.

Agatha was an efficient nurse who anticipated the needs of her patients. She helped many sisters through difficult health problems. She was a cheerful, buoyant, compassionate woman whose competency was deeply respected. Open-minded and generous, she brought out the best in others. Agatha died August 31, 1994 at age 88 after having lived as a Precious Blood sister for 67 years, and as a caring nurse for almost 40 years.

Marian Hall

Within two years of the opening of St. Vincent's, Bishop Joseph Albers of Lansing, Michigan requested that Mother Aquinas open a home for the aging in Flint. He suggested a piece of property, the Flint Tavern Hotel, a six-story building with approximately 200 rooms, in downtown Flint. Bequests and donations enabled the Congregation to purchase it. By the end of 1958, the Sisters of the Precious Blood operated a third facility serving the elderly, which they named Marian Hall.

Sister Christiana (Teresa) Smyth, a former administrator at St. Vincent's, became the first administrator at Marian Hall where she remained from 1958 to 1968. Sister Leonidas Piekenbrock, who had been executive housekeeper at Kneipp Springs for eight years, and Sister Mary George Mouzin made up the first community. With a committed staff, a qualified lay advisory board and the dedicated auxiliary, Marian Hall became a first-rate home for the aged.

Marian Hall was recognized not only for its in-house services, but also for the learning/teaching materials developed on site and still in demand in the early 70s. Though it maintained full occupancy for 25 years, in the mid-1980s two problems surfaced. Because of new emphasis being placed on home health care, the number of applicants began to decline. At the same time, there was a decrease in the number of religious personnel available to serve at Marian Hall. Unable to solve these problems, in 1989 the Congregation engaged Piper Realty to handle the disposition of the property. Eventually, a group known as the Marian Group assumed ownership of the institution.

Lourdes Hall

Mother Nathalia Smith, elected in 1948, moved quickly to address pressing Community needs. One of these was the providing of health care for the growing number of aging sisters. Previously, when sisters in large convents retired, they ordinarily stayed in the convent where they had been living. As a result, aging sisters lived at Maria Stein, New Riegel, Minister, Kneipp Springs, and Salem Heights, with a sister at each place designated as infirmarian or nurse. Increasingly, however, sisters for this task no longer were available. It was time to make a change.

With her characteristic energy and prompt decision-making, Mother Nathalia decided to build a state-of-the-art health care facility for aged and sick sisters. This facility, Lourdes Hall, was to be situated to the west of Salem Heights. Fatima Hall, a high school for girls aspiring to enter the Congregation, had previously been erected on the east side.

Lourdes Hall was to be a three-story building to house 75 sisters with spacious, private rooms. A beautiful chapel, a large recreation room, a dining room and a solarium at the end of each corridor would combine to make Lourdes a

Lourdes Hall

83

pleasant home for aging sisters. Initially, the third floor was reserved for bed patients, and the second, for ambulatory sisters. A pharmacy, an examination room, some treatment rooms and a sterilizing room filled most of the first floor, along with offices and visiting rooms for families of the sisters. Sister Stephana Kamp was named superior of the community at Lourdes.

The new building, a testament to the Congregation's concern for its aged and ill members, opened on April 30, 1952. Gradually, sisters from other Congregational houses were transferred to Lourdes Hall—a difficult move for some who had spent a great portion of their lives in one place. Lourdes, however, provided better care, with doctors and trained nurses to care for them, as well as proximity to hospitals. The first nurses to serve at the new facility included Sisters Venard (Mildred) Westendorf RN, as head nurse; Claudine (Virginia) Hebbeler RN; and Renella Zwick. Sisters Milburgis Lichtenauer, who came with the sisters from Rome City, and Mary Cleophas Schumacher LPN from the Salem Heights infirmary provided additional services as needed. Sisters Innocent (Margaret Mary) Imes RN and Mary Nivard Williams RN, also joined the staff during that first year. At one time or another, most of the Community's sister nurses ministered to aging and elderly sisters at Lourdes Hall.

Sister Mildred (Venard) Westendorf (1914-1995)

Mildred Westendorf, a native of Norwood, Ohio, was the oldest daughter of Joseph and Mary Janning Westendorf. She had one older brother, two younger brothers and two younger sisters. Sadness came to the loving and tight-knit Westendorf family with the death of the mother when Mildred was only 11 years old. Because she was the oldest girl in the family, Mildred dropped out of school after eighth grade to help her father keep the family together. Later, Mildred finished high school at night and then began working at Proctor and Gamble.

In 1934 at age 20, Mildred responded to God's call by joining the Community that had taught her in grade school—the

Sisters of the Precious Blood. Her father, grateful for the generous care she had provided for her younger brothers and sisters, blessed her decision to become a sister.

After her profession, Mildred, who was now Sister Venard, taught for one year at Resurrection School in Dayton and then went into nurses' training at Good Samaritan Hospital in Dayton. After graduating as a registered nurse, she stayed on at the hospital as head nurse in the Women's Geriatric unit. This experience of hospital nursing prepared Venard for the work she would do for most of her life—ministering to sick and aging sisters. In 1944, ten years after she entered, Venard was appointed head nurse in the infirmary at Salem Heights. She endeared herself to postulants, novices and professed alike with her gentle and compassionate manner. One postulant commented, "I not only was sick one day, I was feeling blue, but Sister's gentle care, perception and solicitude provided a mother's touch that did the trick for me. She had a way of knowing what was additionally wrong with you. I never forgot her gifted kindness."

In 1952 she served briefly at Kneipp Springs, followed by a year at Little Flower Academy in San Luis Rey, California as school nurse and substitute teacher. She was instrumental in having a doctor make annual visits for the resident students. At his suggestion, she started a regimen of annual flu shots for the sisters and other staff members, which helped eliminate the usual yearly epidemic.

In 1954 she returned to Lourdes Hall where she served as Director of Nursing for the next ten years. During this time, she also provided in-service training for sisters and lay persons coming into Nursing Arts for the Congregation. From 1964 to 1969, Venard, who changed her name back to Mildred in 1966, served as nurse for residents of Maria Joseph Home, in addition to being superior of the sisters living and working there.

From 1970 through 1973, Mildred was the Director of Nursing for both Lourdes Hall and for the Maria Joseph Home for the Aged. In 1973 at age 60, she retired from full-time ministry in administration and returned to her first love, direct care of patients. She joined the staff first at the Yale Nursing Home in Dayton and later, at the Stillwater Health Center, also in Dayton. Following this, Mildred went to Sacred Heart Parish in New Carlisle, Ohio where she was "on call" to give advice and helpful suggestions to the pastoral staff. As a leisure-time activity, she turned to cooking, something she always enjoyed. On occasion, she invited family and friends to enjoy a meal with her.

Sister Mildred (Venard) Westendorf

In 1988, Mildred retired to Salem Heights where she continued to serve others by volunteering in the pastoral care department of the Maria Joseph Living Care Center. Slowly, she succumbed to failing health, eventually dying from renal infection on July 28, 1995. In Mildred's eulogy, Sister Joyce Lehman, Councilor, said of her, "Her quiet demeanor and compassionate attitude toward patients came from her desire to be a disciple of Jesus, the healer, who not only responded to the pleas of those who came to him, but was also observant of unspoken needs."

Since 1985, the Maria Joseph Living Care Center has made available to the Congregation, for a designated amount, a sufficient number of rooms for Precious Blood sisters who need nursing care. The proximity of the Center to the motherhouse makes it possible for sisters residing at Salem Heights and others in the vicinity to visit and comfort sick and aging sisters. Through pastoral care and friendly visits by its members, the Congregation continues its heritage of care and concern.

Lives of Humble Service

Stories of Sisters Serving
in the Domestic Arts Ministry

By Helen Weber CPPS

Background

Although the Sisters of the Precious Blood from Dayton, Ohio revere Maria Anna Brunner as their foundress, her life with the first sisters was very short. A widow with five grown children, she lived in Switzerland in an old castle, Castle Loewenberg, with her eldest son, Father Francis de Sales Brunner, a priest of the Society of the Precious Blood.

In September of 1833, she returned to Switzerland from a life-changing pilgrimage to Rome imbued with devotion to the Precious Blood of Jesus. The eloquent teaching about the Precious Blood by Gaspar del Bufalo and his colleagues had deeply touched her. Resuming life at the castle, she intensified her life of prayer, adoration of the Blessed Sacrament, and good deeds. Inspired by the depth of her devotion, two maids living at the castle, Elizabeth Meisen and Salome Wasmer, asked to join in her prayers and works of charity. These three women formed the nucleus of the fledgling Community.

Over the next two years, other women affiliated themselves with the small group living at the castle. Soon there

Maria Anna Brunner gathered together the first members of her Community at Castle Loewenburg in Switzerland.

were enough women to begin adoration of the Blessed Sacrament during the night and to expand their charitable works. There is no record of the exact number of Community members by the time of Maria Anna's death on January 15, 1836. Although the women living at the castle shared an ordered life, it is doubtful that Mother Brunner realized in her lifetime that she had founded a religious Community.

From its beginning, Maria Anna's eldest son, Father Francis de Sales, a former Benedictine monk, served as spiritual director and superior of the tiny Community. He prescribed a daily order of prayer and work, *ora et labora*, fashioned on a monastic way of life. Mother Brunner was grateful that, in addition to Francis de Sales being a priest, another son, Joseph, was also studying for the priesthood. She exhorted her spiritual daughters to reverence the priesthood, to pray for priests daily, and to serve them whenever possible. When Father Francis de Sales established a seminary at Castle Loewenberg, his mother and her devoted followers assumed responsibility for cooking and housekeeping. Honoring the Precious Blood of Jesus through prayer and various kinds of work was the goal of the young Community.

Swiss Work Ethic

The Congregation originated in an area of Switzerland containing an integrated population of Swiss, French and German origin. The first women who joined Mother Brunner came from one or other of these groups. The Benedictine mandates of prayer and work fit well into the culturally accepted values—a sense of duty and the importance of hard work—of the Swiss and German people.

The Germanic work ethic and the Benedictine tradition of prayer and work became the twin foundations and, later, the hallmark of the Sisters of the Precious Blood. The influence of Father Brunner's Benedictine formation on the naturally energetic hard-working women prepared them well for the missionary life in America they were soon to undertake. Even though Mother Brunner and the early sisters lived in a castle, there was never anything royal about the way they lived. *Not with Silver or Gold*, the history of the Sisters of the Precious Blood, describes their life:

> At an early hour they said morning prayers in common, in which devotions to the Precious Blood held a prominent place. . . . During the day there was work—hard work: domestic tasks inside the castle and outside labor in the garden, woods, and field. Beautiful vestments for chapel were wrought by deft fingers, clothes were made for the community and for the needy. Whatever the task, it was hallowed by the spirit of recollection and prayer, the golden thread of religious silence running through all the busy hours (p. 62).

The Sisters in America

Father Brunner, who began missionary work in America in 1843, arranged for three sisters to join him there. Volume III of the *CPPS Legacy Series* provides a detailed description of the difficulties facing the sisters when they arrived in pioneer Ohio in 1844. Hard work was essential for survival. The pioneers depended solely upon their own skill and industry to make their farms and villages thrive. The sisters worked extremely hard and, of necessity, acquired skills unknown to them in Europe.

Although the sisters' work was considerably more difficult in pioneer Ohio, they continued the heritage of *ora et labora*. Even after the number of sisters sharing in the labors increased, some were always needed to tend to the more humble duties. In the assignment of tasks, superiors tried to match the talents, skills, and physical strength of the sisters with the work at hand. There was much to be done, and all the sisters shared in the work to the best of their ability. Sisters went joyfully to fields, gardens, kitchens, laundry, classrooms and sewing rooms to praise God through their work.

As the Congregation grew and added new ministries, especially when it expanded its ministry of teaching, the need for some sisters to devote their lives to homemaking

*The hard work of the early sisters made it possible
for the Community to thrive.*

remained. With many sisters teaching for little pay, the Community faced the heavy burden of acquiring funds to purchase necessities. Unlike some communities, the sisters did not beg for their sustenance. They accepted whatever was offered to them as recompense for their work. They also sought alternative and ingenious ways to bring in revenue. Sister Cordelia Gast CPPS described many of these in the first volume of the *CPPS Heritage Series*, "The Work of Their Hands." Cordelia built on the following entry in *Not With Silver or Gold*:

> The Sisters [in America] not engaged in teaching were employed in occupations so varied as to make the Congregation largely self-supporting. Besides working their extensive gardens and fields and plying the usual domestic tasks, they engaged in such handicrafts as spinning, weaving, knitting and shoemaking. Their garments were for the most part homespun; their shoes and hose were their own manufacture. . . . Deft hands fashioned vestments and colorful silk or paper flowers for churches; straw

hats for men's wear; pieces of embroidery. Usually such articles, as well as surplus farm products, were sold for cash or bartered for commodities that could not be supplied at home (p. 151).

Food preparation

The work of sisters assigned to prepare the food was never done! Early in the morning they arose to brew the coffee or some other mixture of grain to fortify the sisters for their hard life. The sister-cooks would then begin making bread for the day. While the bread was rising, they joined the Community in chapel for morning praise, reciting Precious Blood prayers with heartfelt reliance upon God. When a priest was available, they would assist at Mass.

While the other sisters remained in chapel for a quiet thanksgiving, the cooks returned to the kitchen to prepare breakfast. They fried corn mush prepared the previous evening, along with some salt pork. The sisters were not concerned about cholesterol; they knew only that they must supply sufficient food to provide their bodies with the energy necessary to do the work. There was constant concern that the sisters receive adequate and healthful food to prevent illness and disease, such as the dreaded cholera, flu or tuberculosis.

The work of the sister-cooks was never done.

After breakfast the sister cooks attended to the milk obtained earlier by other sisters. They took the milk to the underground cellar to be cooled. In a few hours, after the cream had risen to the top and congealed, they churned it into butter. If the milk soured because it was old or warm, they used it to make cottage cheese.

Sisters working in the fields and gardens brought in vegetables that needed to be used immediately or stored in root cellars—partially underground facilities that maintained food at an even temperature. When the sugar cane was ready, sisters undertook the huge task of making the molasses needed for sweetening. This required many hands, and all the sisters worked together.

The task of supplying provisions for the sisters continued year round. Grain grown in the fields was ground into flour or fed to the cattle and pigs. The sisters hauled hay that had been cut and dried into barns as feed for livestock. Cattle provided milk and milk products. Pigs supplied smoked hams, bacon, sausage or side meat which the sisters "fried down" and stored in its own fat in crockery made by the sisters from the local clay. Preserved meat that had been butchered during the winter, supplemented by wild game and chicken, provided protein for the sisters from winter to winter. All the sisters helped with these preservation processes, just as they all worked in the fields and gardens when crops were ready for harvesting.

The life of a sister-cook in the early days of the Community required stamina and creativity. She was expected to use whatever was available and not allow anything to spoil. She had to know how to butcher chickens and grind corn into cornmeal. Often she was required to chop wood for use in the stoves and ovens. She sweltered in the kitchen in summer and had to break ice in the water barrel in winter. She also had to deal with the monotony of the minimal variety of food, as well as the occasional complaints of the sisters. By the end of winter and early spring, there was often nothing on hand except potatoes and corn meal. *Not With Silver or Gold* tells how even Father Brunner got involved with the problem:

The food of the pioneers was of the plainest. Cornmeal seems to have held an important place in their daily diet. On one occasion, when a superioress complained to Father Brunner that there was little left for their winter fare except potatoes and corn, he ingenuously suggested a variety of recipes for serving the corn, assuring the Sisters that one was more palatable than the other and that the variety of concoctions would be sure to please the most fastidious (p. 152).

Later, as convents acquired some conveniences such as electricity, the life of a sister-cook became somewhat easier. But sisters assigned to the kitchen had to be creative, strong and generous in sharing their talents with the local community. The history of the Congregation tells of hundreds of such women about whom, like many of their companions who were teachers, very little is known.

On the missions

In America, Father Brunner established an interdependent community of priests, sisters and brothers. He called upon the women to provide domestic services for the men. The priests, in turn, celebrated the sacraments for the sisters. The brothers did much of the heavy labor, such as clearing land, building, and farming. Although many sisters helped in the fields during harvest time, most sisters engaged in what had been known in native Switzerland as "women's work." They cleaned the living quarters of the priests and brothers. In addition to preparing meals, they sewed, laundered and mended the men's clothing.

Priests and brothers lived close to nearly all the early convents, thus fulfilling the dream of Father Brunner that the Community live like the Holy Family. This arrangement, however, came to an end in 1878 as a result of a decree from Rome calling for the separation of male and female communities (*Not With Silver or Gold*, p. 233).

Not long after that, in 1879, Father Henry Drees at St. Charles Seminary in Carthagena, Ohio asked Mother Kunigunda Wehrle to send sisters to take over the domestic work there. Brothers had been performing these tasks, but it can be assumed that the men remembered fondly the devoted services of the sisters. For the first time, the sisters took over domestic services away from their established convents.

In 1896 Precious Blood priests at both St. Joseph's College in Collegeville, Indiana and St. Mary's Novitiate in Burkettsville, Ohio requested and received sisters to serve as housekeepers and cooks. The quiet, hard-working sisters viewed their work serving priests and seminarians in these institutions as a privilege. Many of them spoke of their great joy when they received the first blessings of the newly-ordained priests. Precious Blood priests fondly remember Sister Mary Joachim (Anna Marie) Schultis who is featured in Volume I of this series. Her story exemplifies the lives of hundreds of sisters who served the priests and brothers over the years.

The sisters' work soon extended to two additional seminaries in the Archdiocese of Cincinnati—St. Gregory's and Mount St. Mary's. Much later, sisters directed the work at St. Thomas Seminary in Denver, Colorado and Immaculate Heart Seminary in San Diego, California. Sister Ludgeria Bellinghausen's service in several of these places, as described in Volume II of this series, is representative of the lives of many sisters.

Besides working in large institutions, many sisters offered service as cooks or homemakers in mission houses attached to parishes where sisters taught in the schools. Often these sisters, being alone all day while the teachers were in school, suffered from loneliness and a sense of isolation. The teachers, however, appreciated the homelike atmosphere created for them by the sister-housekeepers.

Very early in the Congregation's involvement in education, superiors responded to demands that sister-teachers become professionally trained. They devoted time, resources and personnel to this goal (See *CPPS Legacy Series*, Vol. III, pp.

39-58). Unfortunately, the same was not true for sisters assigned to become cooks, housekeepers, or to do other work designated as "domestic." No academic education was provided for them except the opportunity to learn English, if they were foreign born. From 1844 until 1911, when the last European-born sister entered the Congregation, over 300 members came from foreign countries.

Although improvement in the education of sisters in general arts was slow in coming, it did finally come. Through the efforts of Sister Gertrude Ann (Damascene) Droll and Sister Marcella (Agnita) Ensman, sisters began to receive professional training.

Sister Gertrude Ann (Damascene) Droll (1912-1998)

A young nun, only four years in the Community, disembarked the train in Atchison, Kansas on a bright September morning in 1940. Sister Damascene and her companion, Sister Veronita Merkel, politely asked a taxi driver to take them to Mount St. Scholastica College. As the awesome twin towers of the Abbey church came into view, a sense of peace settled over the young women. This lovely college campus, nestled within the bend of the Missouri River, would be their home for the next two years. They would come to love and respect the Benedictine sisters who generously demonstrated their charism of hospitality. Damascene and Veronita were the first two Precious Blood sisters to become professional dietitians.

Damascene, the former Gertrude Ann Droll, was born in Cloverdale, Ohio in 1912. She entered the Sisters of the Precious Blood in 1937 at the age of 24, having acquiesced in her mother's advice to "have a little of life's experiences" before entering. The youngest of eight children, she brought with her to the convent the spirit of joy characteristic of her family.

She often acknowledged that her older brothers and sisters, one of whom, Eva, preceded her in the convent as Sister Leandra, had spoiled her by showering their attention upon her. The love and security she experienced as a child enabled her to provide the same for the many people with whom she would later come in contact.

Sister Gertrude Ann (Damascene) Droll

Kneipp Springs

After completing her training in dietary education in Kansas, followed by an internship at Good Samaritan Hospital in Cincinnati, Damascene was sent to Kneipp Springs in Rome City, Indiana. As the first registered dietitian at the Springs, she immediately began to provide a more professional atmosphere in the culinary department. She changed labor practices in the kitchen: each sister now worked eight-hour days and enjoyed a free day each week. Housekeepers, laundresses, and others at the Springs also benefited from the changes Damascene brought about in the kitchen. Prior to this, the only time off from work given to sisters in domestic arts was for the annual retreat.

Damascene taught the sisters how to prepare balanced menus and nutritious food. In her gentle but thorough way of instructing others, she taught sister-cooks all aspects of meal presentation. She introduced the practice of rotating cooks in the preparation of meats, potatoes and vegetables, salads and desserts, thus giving wide experience to all. This action, typical of Damascene, merged education with practice and produced more professional and more satisfied food service personnel.

During her 23-year tenure in Rome City, Damascene brought about many other changes in the field of culinary arts. She modernized equipment for cooking by replacing coal stoves with gas. Fryers, grills and steam kettles took the place of the huge skillets and pots formerly used for stove-top cooking. She purchased stainless steel table tops and cabinets, a mixer and a refrigerator. She disposed of all chipped dishes and granite pans. She did everything she could to make the work of the sisters easier, as well as the food they prepared more healthful.

Since many sisters ministered at Kneipp Springs at some time in their careers, the results of Damascene's efforts to improve working conditions spread throughout the Congregation. Sisters were no longer expected to work seven days a week or long hours daily. Mother Magna Lehman, who had been elected in 1936, placed great emphasis upon the need for better living conditions and more healthful life styles for the sisters. These goals were, in great part, realized by Damascene working quietly out of her little diet kitchen at Kneipp Springs.

Gertrude Ann knew the secret of how to relax.

Later years

Damascene left Rome City in 1966 when she was appointed Regional Director for the Northern Region of the Congregation. To this position she brought her warm, caring personality and her desire to improve the quality of the lives of the sisters. The Region benefited from her deep affection for the sisters and her enormous capacity to listen, as well as from her love for parties and her famous fudge. At some time during these years, Damascene returned to her baptismal name of Gertrude Ann and was affectionately called "Gertie."

When her five-year term as Regional Director ended in 1971, Gertrude Ann became director of the diet kitchen in the Clio Convalescent Center in Clio, Michigan. She remained there for 14 years residing at St. Pius X convent in Flint, Michigan where she was a welcome and cherished presence.

Following major surgery, Gertie retired from dietary work at age 73 and went to Salem Heights Motherhouse in Dayton, Ohio. For the next 13 years, as her health slowly deteriorated, she continued to spread warmth and love. Her kind heart finally gave out on July 28, 1998.

Sister Marcella (Agnita) Ensman (1909-1994)

The curtains on the convent windows in Russia, Ohio rippled limply in the hot humid air. The sisters who were gathered around the study table appreciated even a slight breeze as they created lesson plans for classes in home economics. Entering the room with a tray of tall glasses of lemonade, their hostess, Sister Agnita Ensman, urged the sisters to take a break from their studies to have a cool drink. This was the third summer that the Congregation's home economic teachers spent a week together developing their curriculum. In 1948, home economics was a relatively new teaching field for sisters, and this sharing of experience was enriching for them.

The home economics teachers recognized Agnita as a leader and creative organizer. She had become a respected and experienced dietary and clothing teacher. It was no surprise to them when, in 1951, Mother Nathalia Smith, who succeeded

Mother Magna, appointed her to be the first supervisor of general arts personnel. The work of improving the living conditions of the sisters, begun by Mother Magna, received a strong mandate in the Chapter of 1948. Mother Nathalia, the former novice mistress, was well aware of the need for ongoing formation for sisters, both in their religious life commitment and in their professional expertise. *More Than the Doing* notes the appointment of Agnita:

> [Mother Nathalia's] appointment of Sister Marcella [Agnita] Ensman, an experienced high school home economics teacher as Supervisor of Domestic Arts, was consistent with the mandate of improved educational preparation. Marcella provided support services for home-making staffs in convents and institutions, and she arranged for these Sisters to obtain professional education in their fields of service (p. 74).

As mentioned previously, superiors for many years had encouraged and provided learning opportunities for the teaching sisters. Since 1899, school supervisors had the responsibility of helping teachers become professional, better educated and more skilled instructors. Now, over 50 years later, the Congregation finally addressed, in a formal way, the needs of the sisters in general arts.

In her new role, Agnita immediately began to send members of domestic departments for professional educational experiences. She provided support services through newsletters and visits to sisters serving in convents and in institutions. She offered workshops, usually conducted by Precious Blood sisters, in various places. Among the topics included were communication skills, personal growth and development, nutrition and proper care in cleaning, and the preparation and preservation of foods.

Sisters who were laundresses now went to programs for institutional laundry managers. Sister-cooks attended seminars about foods and diets; those working with the elderly

Sister Marcella (Agnita) Ensman

attended presentations on various topics connected with service to seniors. Housekeepers met their peers as they learned about the latest methods and the equipment used in maintaining institutions. Through further academic education, many sisters received opportunities to realize their professional potential.

Other opportunities

St. Joseph's College in Rensselaer, Indiana, where Sisters of the Precious Blood already staffed the culinary department, provided an interesting experience enjoyed by a number of sisters. The college hired Miss Helen Skinner, a professional dietitian, to provide education and assistance to sisters serving in the kitchen. In 1951 the college offered a program using the facilities at the college as a working lab for culinary arts personnel from various religious communities. Mother Nathalia, recognizing this as an opportunity for the professional development of sister-cooks, sent three sisters to take part in it.

Religious from other congregations also participated in this program. At the end of the summer, the superior of the Franciscans sisters from Sylvania, Ohio asked if two of their members could stay at the college for an extended experience of working with the sisters in the kitchen. The mixture of college professionals and sister-kitchen workers under the capable leadership of Miss Skinner proved to be a model for similar experiences elsewhere.

By the time Mother Mary Aquinas Stadtherr became the major superior of the Congregation in 1954, many of the sisters in general arts had taken part in study opportunities. Agnita continued to encourage sisters in their professional development. This trend continued over the next two decades. When Agnita was superior at the motherhouse, the college at Salem Heights offered a program of studies for novices and young professed who were not preparing to be teachers. Courses such as Public Speaking and Personality Development provided a valuable background for further study. Sisters attended St. Louis University for training in a relaxed but professional educational atmosphere. Sisters in general arts continued to attend national and regional conventions and workshops. They shared their experiences with their peers in a regular newsletter entitled *C.PP.S. Professional Highlights*. The Congregation encouraged them to join professional organizations, and some served as officers in state and national associations. Congregational publications celebrated sisters who received degrees and honors.

When the Congregation in August, 1954 made the decision to change to a gray habit, Agnita took on a challenging project. She directed the entire process of providing new habits for over 800 sisters and novices within one year. Though many sisters assisted in this enormous undertaking, Agnita probably cut out most of the habits herself! On August 22, 1955, sisters in all parts of the country simultaneously changed from black wool habits to habits of gray Dacron.

Agnita lived at Salem Heights from 1951 to 1966; she was superior of the house for six of those years. She enjoyed planning parties for the sisters. She was a creative cook, and she delighted in designing special table settings and menus. She taught herself to decorate cakes and took pleasure in decorating hundreds of them. She also excelled in a variety of artistic crafts, such as crocheting and knitting.

Later years

In 1966, oversight of the general arts personnel became the responsibility of Sister Leonita Westerheide, a member of the General Council, relieving Agnita of many of her responsibilities. At this time, Agnita returned to her baptismal name, Marcella. Now 57 years old, she resumed teaching home economics in the high school in Russia, Ohio. Ten years later, she retired from teaching but remained in Russia to prepare meals for the sisters. Later, she cooked in the convents in Maria Stein and Celina, Ohio, while spending her free time working on various crafts.

Marcella returned to Dayton in 1991, at age 81. She could take pride in her long and active involvement in the lives of the sisters. Because of her leadership, many sisters in general arts could now proudly display academic credentials. Even more important, thanks to her, these sisters had become more

Marcella excelled in cake-decorating and other crafts.

confident and self-assured in their ministry. Although she was not alone in advancing the professional development of sisters, she was a pivotal person in the process. In her 15 years as Director of Domestic Arts, she helped to make up for the dearth of educational opportunities provided over the previous 100 years. Due to the work of Gertrude Ann and Marcella, the Community began to recognize more fully the valuable contributions sisters in general arts make to the life and well-being of the Congregation.

Many hundreds of sisters spent their entire lives in ministries of humble service, yet little is recorded of their dedication. Often, only their name on a Congregational roster indicates their presence in the Community. Within the last half-century, however, more detailed records have become available. The stories of the following two sisters, Sister Regina (Honorata) Maas and Sister Praxedes Karalfa, provide a sampling of the lives of sisters in general arts. Selected primarily because of the availability of data concerning them in the archives, they represent hundreds of others whose stories also deserve telling.

Sister Regina (Honorata) Maas (1903-1998)

Cloverdale, a tiny, peaceful village on the flat farmlands of northwestern Ohio, was the birthplace of Sister Regina Maas. Lying mostly along State Route 114, Cloverdale has little business and no industry. Today, people go to Cloverdale primarily to visit loved ones in Paradise Oaks Nursing Home on the edge of town. The majority of its less-than-300 resident population are descendants of German immigrants who came into the area over 100 years ago to clear the land and break up the resistant soil for farming.

From the beginning, farming has been the principal economy of the area. Today, the village has two major streets, running perpendicular to each other. Along the main street, one would now pass the post office, a beauty/barber shop, a couple of bars, and a former hardware store converted into a computer and electronics shop. Turning the corner onto the other street, a visitor comes upon the Catholic church, the parish center (formerly the school), and a stately brick residence that once housed the sisters who taught in the school.

Over the past 50 years, there have been quite a few changes in the village. In the bustling days of the 1950s, the village had two churches, Catholic and Protestant; two schools, Catholic and public; a grocery; a drug store; a hardware store; and a town hall. Only the lovely Catholic church, the post office and the saloons remain today.

Father Michael Mueller, pastor of neighboring Ottoville in 1898, recognized early on that Catholics settling in the area around Cloverdale faced a real hardship. It was necessary for them to travel about eight miles to Ottoville for Mass, no small distance by horse and buggy. To remedy this, Father Mueller founded St. Barbara's parish in Cloverdale. He celebrated Mass there every other week and asked the bishop to appoint a permanent pastor for the fledgling parish. And permanent, the appointee proved to be! Father Henry Wickman served as pastor of the Cloverdale parish from 1900 until 1942!

Until 1966, the village took pride in its Catholic school. In order to serve children of German immigrants, the parish, in

Early St. Barbara's Church in Cloverdale, Ohio

1904, invited the Sisters of the Precious Blood to staff the new school. St. Barbara's, with Sister Mary Agnes Hammer as the first superior and principal, numbered only about 100 children, but both parents and children enthusiastically supported the school. Students advancing to public high schools from St. Barbara's possessed a strong academic background. When the sisters withdrew 62 years later, the school closed. Consolidation of public schools by the state sometime later left Cloverdale without a school.

One of the greatest claims to fame for this predominantly Catholic rural area is the large number, per capita, of young women entering religious communities. The Sisters of the Precious Blood were the recipients of some of its finest. Twenty-one Precious Blood sisters have proudly proclaimed Cloverdale as their home town. The story of Sister Gertrude Ann (Damascene) Droll appears earlier in this volume. In addition to Sister Regina (Honorata) Maas whose story follows, her sister, Sister Hilaria, is included in Volume III of this series. Volume III also relates the story of Sister Barbara Webken, another daughter of the parish. Two former major superiors of the Congregation, Mother Nathalia Smith and Sister Joyce Langhals, also called Cloverdale home.

The Maas family

Like many other German immigrants coming to the United States in the late 19th century, the Maas family arrived with little cash, but a great deal of determination. By the turn of the century, the family managed to increase the size of its farm from 40 to 80 acres. The ground was primarily tough clay needing great effort to make it productive, but Charles and Anna Maas and their children made an ample living from it.

All the Maas children who lived beyond infancy—three boys and five girls—grew up understanding the importance of hard work. The youngest child, born on March 23, 1903, received the name Regina, meaning *queen*. Cherished by her older brothers and sisters, she, nevertheless, soon learned that even *queens* must share in the tasks necessary to maintain such a large family.

In 1906, when Regina was only three, her 14-year-old sister, Josephine, entered the Congregation of the Sisters of the Precious Blood at Maria Stein, Ohio. Both keenly felt the separation. Sixteen years later, when Regina also joined the Community, they would have the opportunity to get to know each other as adults. When Josephine left home, the other children had filled in with the work, as was expected. Because Regina had many older siblings, one might suppose she had less responsibility and fewer chores around the farm. Apparently, this was not the case since throughout her life she demonstrated the values of hard work and fulfilling of obligations, regardless of personal demands.

As was the custom at that time, farm children often completed their education at grade eight and began to assume adult responsibilities. After completing her education at St. Barbara's, Regina remained at home helping with work around the house and on the farm. Very probably, like many adolescent girls of the period, she also assisted other families with new babies or elderly relatives needing care.

Honorata (right), as a very young sister, poses with her sister, Hilaria.

Religious life

At some point during her teenage years, Regina felt God calling her to become a religious. When she was 19, she followed Josephine, then called Sister Mary Hilaria, into the convent at Maria Stein, entering on September 4, 1922. Within a month, the new class of postulants moved to the new motherhouse in Dayton, Ohio. As a postulant and a novice, Regina pursued high school studies. At investiture, she received the name of Sister Mary Honorata. After the Chapter of 1966, she returned to her baptismal name of Regina.

Following profession of temporary vows on August 15, 1925, Honorata worked as a housekeeper at the Fenwick Club, a boarding place for young men and boys working in Cincinnati, Ohio. She stayed there until 1927 when she was sent to Kneipp Sanitarium in Rome City, Indiana to help with nursing. After only a few weeks there, one of the sister-cooks needed surgery, and the superior asked Honorata to fill in for her. Because Honorata proved to be such an excellent cook, this three-week assignment extended to 50 years as a cook at Kneipp Springs, in seminaries, and in other large institutions. Reflecting back on this time much later, she commented, *They told me that you don't take a good cook out of the kitchen!* When asked if she liked the change, she responded in her good-natured, straight-forward style, *I did what needed to be done. It didn't make any difference to me.*

Labor of love

From 1927 to 1936, Honorata prepared thousands of meals for the residents and the sisters at Kneipp Sanitarium. She was a large woman, very strong and capable of handling the heavy pots and skillets. She could scramble dozens of eggs while keeping an eye on sausage frying. With ease, she could handle the huge roasters full of succulent fried children or tender beef. She was strong and she was competent.

Most of all, however, people remember Honorata for her quiet demeanor even at difficult times. In her humble way, she handled the pressures of her position. During the tense moments before serving guests, when many cooks became agitated, she calmly went about her work. Her round face might redden from the heat of the stove, but never from temper or frustration.

During her 54 years of work in large institutions, Regina at times bore the responsibility of being kitchen supervisor and superior of the sisters. In these roles, her relationships with the sisters were loving, generous, cheerful and accepting of others and their opinions. An unnamed younger sister acknowledged her debt to her in this way: "Regina was a mentor for me, even though I didn't understand the term at the time. She was like a mother, guiding me, helping me, giving me courage to make a success of myself."

Regina was especially fond of her work in the seminaries. She loved to tell about the priests she knew when they were adolescents in the minor seminary and the novitiate or as aspiring young theologians at St. Charles Seminary in Carthagena, Ohio. Among her treasured memories were the first blessings of the newly ordained.

Congregational archives reveal very little about Regina. However, when interviewed and recorded on audio tape by Sister Florentine Gregory, she recounted the following incident: One time Mother Magna Lehman asked her what she thought about a retreat she had just made at St. Charles. She replied, *I didn't make retreat. Oh, if you mean last week, then I guess we are always in retreat around here. The only difference was that during that retreat we ran up and down the steps for all the conferences and did all our work, too.* Regina obviously got her point across. After that, sisters working at St. Charles and other seminaries no longer made retreats at the places where they worked.

Regina's later days

After laboring for years in the kitchens of Kneipp Springs, St. Joseph College, St. Charles Seminary, Burkettsville Novitiate and Lourdes Hall in Dayton, revisiting some places several times, she eventually retired to the motherhouse at Salem Heights in January of 1979 at age 76. She was still strong, but the years had taken their toll.

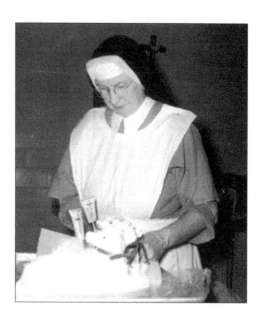

Regina, an excellent cook, prepares a lamb cake for a Paschal celebration.

During the following nine years, she spent much of her time praying and relaxing with her sisters. She also loved to work in the gardens around the convent. Her rural background had imbued her with a love of nature and a delight in watching things grow. When her health failed in 1988, she moved to Emma Hall, the Congregation's nursing care facility, where she lived for another ten years. Her strong body and indomitable spirit gradually weakened, and she died peacefully at age 95.

Only God knows the number of meals Regina prepared and how many people went away from her meals fully satisfied. Her strong hands, her cheerful and quiet disposition, and her unselfish dedication to service caused many to recognize that Regina, *queen of the kitchen,* was also a royal example of humble and dedicated service to others.

Sister Mary Praxedes Karalfa (1902-1966)

On Monday afternoons in the 1940s and 50s, white-veiled novices walked hurriedly, but quietly, to the laundry in Salem Heights convent. Their religious instruction over for the day, they would now spend an hour working in the usually hot and steamy laundry.

Before the novices arrived, Sister Praxedes Karalfa, the sister-in-charge, had all in readiness for them. Not a moment would be wasted. When they entered the large room with its huge washing machines, industrial-sized mangle and dryer, several presses, and many ironing boards and folding tables, she greeted them warmly. In her usual efficient manner, she matched each novice to a particular task.

Novices with long arms took their places at the mangle to iron bed linens. Two fed the damp sheets into the mangle while four others removed them on the opposite side and folded them in a very precise manner. Another group used the

Sister Praxedes Karalfa

presses for flat pieces. Still others ironed starched collars, the most skilled being entrusted with the linens of the superiors. The remaining novices folded piles of underwear and towels.

Never embarrassing anyone, Praxedes occasionally told a novice quietly that a task needed to be done over. She supervised the young women in a caring, non-dictatorial manner. Although the work was sometimes tedious, most novices enjoyed this time of disciplined activity. The laundry offered opportunity for novices to relate to a professed sister other than those in the novitiate.

One may wonder how Praxedes was able to match people to tasks so well. Her method was simple. Having carefully observed the young women when they were aspirants and postulants, by the time they were novices, she had assessed each one's strengths. She was ready to assign a suitable task to each novice. What, in Praxedes' background, might have prepared her for this kind of supervisory role?

Elizabeth Agnes Karalfa

Among the nine children born to Hungarian immigrants, Joseph Andrew Karalfa and Mary Barbara Szabo, was Elizabeth Agnes, who would one day be known as Sister Praxedes. She came into the world on June 12, 1902 in the industrial town of Johnstown, Pennsylvania. It is not known when her parents came to Johnstown, or if they were living there at the time of the devastating flood of 1889 when over 2,000 people died. Records indicate that Betty, as Elizabeth Agnes was known to her family, lived in Johnstown at least until she received the sacrament of Confirmation in 1912, at age 10.

Betty attended the Johnstown public schools. While she was a teenager, her family moved to Cleveland where they joined Our Lady of Good Counsel Parish and became part of the Hungarian community in the area. Prior to her entrance into the Precious Blood Community at 36, Betty possibly had minimal contact with the Sisters of the Precious Blood who taught in the parish school.

The May Company, an outstanding department store in Cleveland, hired Betty and, recognizing her natural abilities, promoted her to the position of floor lady. In this job, she developed the skill to evaluate the abilities of those under her direction and to make assignments based on her assessment. This experience no doubt accounts for her uncanny ability to match novices with appropriate tasks in the laundry at Salem Heights. Other than her work at the May Company, little is known of her life prior to 1939 when she sought entrance into the Congregation of the Sisters of the Precious Blood. Her personnel file contains a letter of recommendation written by her pastor, Father Sebastian Kremer, in 1936:

> Dear Mother Magna,
> [I] am glad to recommend to you as a candidate for your Congregation Betty Karalfa. She is a lady of fine personality and character. She has genuine piety, is charitable and generous, and receives the sacraments very frequently. Her determination to stay [in the convent] is strong. If you do not accept her, she'll try somewhere else. She has worked for years at the May Co. Dept. Store and thus learned to handle and get along with people. Though her age is 36, she does not look it, and [her age] ought not keep her from entering the convent. [At that time women beyond the age of 30 were ordinarily not admitted to the Congregation.]
> She has ever been healthy. I do not know of any insanity, or hereditary sickness in her family. Almost her entire family are good, practical Catholics. . . .
>
> Sincerely yours in C.PP.S.
> Father [Sebastian] Kremer

Betty Karalfa entered the Congregation on June 29, 1939. When she was invested as a novice on August 15, 1940, she received the name of Sister Mary Praxedes. After her two years' novitiate, she was assigned to work in the infirmary at Salem Heights, followed by one year of domestic work at St. Gregory's Seminary in Cincinnati, Ohio. She then returned to Dayton to begin her 14-year tenure as laundress at Salem

Heights. Since laundry work occupied only a few days each week, Praxedes also worked in the altar bread department. Making use of her background in business, she kept accounts and supervised the mailing of altar breads to customers.

Fond recollections

Many sisters remember Praxedes primarily for her work in the Motherhouse laundry. Though her work was demanding, she maintained a pleasant demeanor. The laundry was usually hot, with washing machines, dryers, irons and presses all pouring hot air into the large room. In winter it felt cozy and comfortable, but in hot, humid Ohio in the summertime with no air-conditioning, the place became stifling. But as one sister who worked in the laundry as a novice recalled, "There was absolutely no complaining about the heat, which seemed over 100 degrees."

Praxedes was always a hard worker, one who labored more diligently than those under her direction. She insisted on handling all the heavy work—pulling clothes from the laundry tubs and putting them into the spinner or the dryer—by herself.

Praxedes spent a good portion of her life directing work in laundries.

117

Sisters who knew Praxedes recall her sense of humor and her story-telling ability. Sister Alma Catherine Huelskamp, who lived with Praxedes as a novice and later at St. Gregory's, says, "Praxedes was a delightful community member and a fun-loving person." Though it was not customary for sisters at that time to speak of their families, Praxedes often told stories about hers. Community members chuckled when Praxedes talked about her little nephew. Once when he was old enough to observe his mother breast feeding a new baby, but too young to understand, he screamed frantically, "The baby is eating his mommy!" Praxedes loved entertaining her sisters with tales like this, and they enjoyed it.

Many sisters who were novices between 1946 and 1960 have memories of working in the laundry with Praxedes. They observed her firsthand cheerfully performing demanding work. They also watched her demonstrate enormous capability of organization and astute personnel management in an unobtrusive manner.

Other assignments

In 1960 Praxedes became assistant administrator with Sister Mary Grace Pratt at the Maria Joseph Home, adjacent to Salem Heights. A year later, she received an assignment to do domestic work, including laundry, at Little Flower Academy, in San Luis Rey, California. Never having had the opportunity to see much of the United States, this was an exciting move for her. She relished the experiences of picnicking on the beach, picking oranges off a tree, and enjoying the delightful climate of Southern California.

After only three years at the Academy, Praxedes moved to Kneipp Springs, in Rome City, Indiana to do domestic work and to supervise women working as maids and waitresses. Because of her background supervising women at the May Company, this seemed like a perfect match for Praxedes. However, because she was already feeling the early effects of the cancer that eventually took her life, her time in Rome City proved to be very short. She remained there only one year.

Praxedes' last days

While at Kneipp Springs, Praxedes suffered from shingles in her mouth. Treatment failed to control the development of the disease, and in 1965, Praxedes moved to Lourdes Hall, the Congregation's infirmary in Dayton. Soon after, her doctor diagnosed her condition as cancer of the tongue and throat. Suffering filled the last months of her life, and doctors sent her for care to Christ Hospital in Cincinnati. Typically, she made light of her situation, saying the cancer came from "all the unwashed apples I've eaten." The notice of her death in the Congregation's newsletter (April, 1966), says:

> Sister Mary Praxedes died a victim of cancer of the tongue and throat at Christ Hospital, Cincinnati, Ohio, on February 25, 1966, shortly after she had received Holy Communion. She had been taken there from Lourdes Hall Infirmary the week before to undergo a second series of treatments, to which she was not responding. To the end she was a model patient, though the sufferings she endured during the previous months must have been excruciating. She was offering them, she was heard to say, for Krushchev that he might find mercy with God.

Praxedes lived only 26 years as a member of the Congregation. Her life was largely unnoticed and unheralded. On the application form before entering the Community, in answer to the question, "Why do you wish to enter the convent?" she had written in her strong, womanly script, *To give myself in the service of God and for my own sanctity.* God took her at her word and accepted her brief 26 years of service. The announcement of her death, at age 64, summed up her life in this way:

> Always cheerful, ever ready with the funny anecdote or joke, apt at whatever job she put her hand, prayerful to the end, Sister Mary Praxedes

lived her life in total dedication and faced death with courage and resignation to God's Holy Will. May she rest in peace!

The lives of sisters in domestic arts were usually simple and undramatic. A special privilege enjoyed by most of them was the honor of spending a daily hour of prayer and adoration before the Blessed Sacrament. This contemplative time, plus the simplicity of their lifestyle, assisted them in their quest for personal holiness. Many attained deep spirituality through *ora et labora*, prayer and work. Most often, their inner lives were known only to God, but sometimes, God intervened in the life of a special individual. Such a person was Sister Mary Ildephonsa Gschwind. In 1938 an unnamed superior, recognizing in her one of these privileged persons, told her to write the story of her life. Her autobiography provides the framework of the following story.

Sister Ildephonsa Gschwend (1852-1942)

A soft click broke the silence of the night as a tiny, stooped woman opened and slipped through the chapel door. Bright lights, focused on the glittering golden monstrance enthroned on the altar, dispelled the darkness of the chapel. All was quiet. The little old nun knew that above her in the choir loft were sisters deep in silent worship. But nothing mattered to her except the powerful attraction of Love drawing her toward the altar.

Quietly moving through the side chapel to the center of the altar rail, she knelt reverently on the prie-dieu used for daytime adoration. From that close vantage point, she gazed lovingly at the Sacred Host exposed on the high altar. Recessed spotlights intensified the gold and white of the altar, the white lilies gracing the steps on either side, and the candles flickering tranquilly. Oblivious of all this beauty, Sister Ildephonsa Gschwend's eyes focused on the monstrance alone.

The clock in the choir loft softly chimed two a.m. as the sisters, recently awakened from sleep, arrived to begin a new hour of adoration. Together with the sisters who had prayed the previous hour, they intoned the opening prayer. Then, silently, the earlier group left, as subdued voices began to pray the rosary. On the chapel floor below, already in rapturous communion with her God, Ildephonsa was deep in contemplation of the Divine Presence.

Background

Mary Gschwend had left Switzerland in 1882, at age 30, to join the Sisters of the Precious Blood in Maria Stein, Ohio. In addition to being older than the average applicant, she differed in other ways from most of the young women entering the Community at that time. She was educated, and she had traveled in many European countries. She had acquired knowledge and skill in five languages: German, English, Latin, French and Italian.

When she was 86 years old, her superior directed her to write the story of her life thus far. Humbly she obeyed and began her account in this way:

Motherhouse, Dayton, Ohio
1938

PRAISED BE JESUS CHRIST

The destinies of men* and the vocations to which men are called by the good and almighty Father in Heaven are so manifold, that it seems to me, no two persons among the millions in this world, travel exactly the same road through life. Oh, wonderful Omnipotence and Providence of God, how inimitable Thou art! My life's journey also is a riddle; in so strange a manner, and yet so mercifully and lovingly was I led by the All High God. . . . I was really led by Divine Providence in a wonderful way. . . .

In spite of my limited intellectual ability, I always aimed at becoming great, at doing things worthwhile, but this was not according to God's plan. I had abundant opportunity for acquiring knowledge in all possible branches of learning and art, but talent was missing. I was to remain small and lowly. My good Father in Heaven, however, led me in a wonderful way.

I was born and baptized on the 23rd of September, 1852, at Altstatten, Ct. St. Gall, Switzerland. My father's name was Joseph Gschwend, and my dead, good mother's name was Anna Eugster. My father had a bakery. We lived on Angel Street (Engelgasse) a few steps only from the parish church.

I have always had the grace to live near a church, and I have associated with saints, even such as have been raised to the altars. I have seen and admired the finest palaces . . . but have always felt that such things cannot compare with the heavenliness and richness of a parish church or convent.

*Inclusive language was not common usage at that time.

When Mary was a very young child, her mother died. It was her mother's dying wish that the little girl would live with a neighbor. Since there is no mention of her father at this time or later, it is evident that he was either already deceased or, at least, unable to care for her.

The Shrine of Maria Stein in Switzerland

Leaving Switzerland

Mary's young life seems to have been a period of wandering. After some time with the above-mentioned neighbor, another of her mother's friends, who had married an Italian, took the child with her to Italy. No reason is given for this transfer to a second unnamed guardian. She remained in Italy for several years during which time she learned to speak Italian. From Italy she went to France. Of this period of her life, she wrote:

> *From there [Italy] I went to Nice, where I learned the French language. I have traveled through many countries. I was in Rome, Italy, France and England. I was bound for Ireland one time, but the people and church services in England seemed too cold and chilly to me, that I went back to France. There I found Catholicity and association with holy souls, and also received favors from heaven.*

Why she took these journeys and with whom she traveled is unknown. During the time of her travels through Europe she was probably in her late teens. No doubt she attended school wherever she was at the time.

France

While in France, she entered a convent. However, because of the war between Germany and France, she was not allowed to remain in the convent, though she stayed in France. She wrote:

> *No German postulant could be received at this time so I became a nurse-girl in a family of a millionaire. The mother of the little child I cared for was a very good religious woman who had received her education in an Academy of the Madames of the Sacred Heart. I had no other work except the care of one child. These people wanted me to remain always with them, and offered me some fine rooms in their palace, but I was afraid to take the offer, fearing for the welfare of my soul.*

St. Bernadette Soubirous as a young woman

During these years, Mary evidently earned enough money to be rather independent. She worked in a hospital and a boarding school in Nevers, France where Bernadette Soubirous, later canonized by the Church as St. Bernadette, was staying. After her visions at Lourdes, Bernadette had entered the Ursuline convent in 1866 on the recommendation of the Bishop of Lourdes. She was forbidden to talk about the visions and was generally hidden from public view. A special permission was required to meet her.

In 1872 Sister Marie-Bernard (Bernadette) served as a nurse in a military hospital for soldiers injured in the Franco-Prussian War. At the hospital in Nevers, probably around 1875, Mary met Bernadette. Of their meeting, Mary wrote, *Through the intervention of Rev. Father Dosenbach from Felkirch, who knew me as a child, and who happened to be there at the time, I got to see and speak to St. Bernadette, and even helped her work at some curtains.*

Mary stayed in France for a number of years working and earning her living. In her mid-20s, she began to experience special favors from God. She described being in Paris in a wonderful garden that contained little alcoves and grottoes where, she said, *I seemed to see Jesus, sweating blood, and could not help myself from weeping. At another time, I saw the Heavenly Father as you see Him pictured. This time I heard a voice clear and plain. It said, "Come, come to me."* She was very surprised at this experience and did not tell others about it for fear they might think she had lost her mind.

Rome

While in her bedroom early on the morning of December 31, 1877, Mary heard what she believed to be God's voice saying, "Go to Rome." She was astonished since she did not know how to get to Rome, nor did she know anyone there. But the prompting was so powerful that she felt compelled to act upon it. She described her response:

> *I had no rest, however, so at two o'clock of the same day, I was ready for the journey. I had plenty money, and*

New Years, 1878 noon found me across the mountains in Milan. From there I went to Genoa to the sea where I took sail for Rome. I spoke the Italian language fluently, and had myself taken to the church of the Blessed Mother of God. To this church I went day after day, sometimes forgetting about taking meals.

As she awaited further word from God, she boarded with religious women whom she refers to as "Sisters of the Precious Blood." Very probably, they were Adorers of the Blood of Christ, the Community founded by Blessed Maria DeMattias. At that time it was commonplace for unaccompanied young Catholic women to seek accommodations in convents.

Sparked by the American and French revolutions, the spirit of revolution against tyrannical monarchs spreading across Europe reached Italy by the late 19th century. Vatican City did not escape the turmoil, and a series of rebellions against the pope took place. At that time, a large section of Italy, the Papal States, was under the direct control of the

Twice in her young life, Ildephonsa experienced God calling her to Rome.

126

Pope. Pius IX had inherited unrest from his predecessor, Gregory XVI, who had suppressed demands for justice and democracy. Citizens of the Papal States, in open rebellion, welcomed General Guiseppe Garibaldi who forced the Pope's army into submission. Pius IX responded by withdrawing into the Vatican, becoming literally a "Prisoner of the Vatican."

The upheavals in Rome did not prevent Mary from obtaining an audience with the Pope as she had hoped. With the help of the Fathers of the Holy Redeemer, she was granted an audience with Pius IX, shortly before his death on February 7, 1878. Filled with youthful impetuosity and naiveté, she believed he would have a message for her from God. The 86-year-old Pontiff, however, had no special message for her. Soon afterward, Mary decided to leave Rome and go to her brother's home in Switzerland.

Rome, a second time

Her sojourn with her brother's family was short-lived. On the morning of September 23 of the following year, 1879, she again heard the call, "You must go to Rome!" Immediately complying, she boarded a train for Italy by early afternoon that same day feeling *happy as a little child.*

Once again in Rome, most probably staying with the Sister Adorers, she resolved to see the Pope, still firmly believing that he would have God's message for her. Redemptorist priests again arranged an audience for her with the new Pope, Leo XIII, who presented her with some medals, including a large one especially for her. The Pontiff, however, gave her no special message from God. Although she did not remain very long in Rome, she fondly recalled an experience from that time:

> *. . . I met Don Bosco while I was there. He even asked me whether I would sew a surplice for him. He gave me the goods. Although I did not know how to go about cutting and sewing it for him, still I could not refuse, as he was so friendly. I, therefore, took the bundle and in my dilemma*

sought help from the Sisters. . . . One of the Sisters cut and sewed it for me, while I helped a little with the sewing. Then we took it to Don Bosco, telling him that we both worked on it, and he paid us for the work. He would not have it any other way.

Mary then returned to her brother's home in Switzerland. His family, she relates, *was very good and very religious.* A son, Mary's nephew, was a priest, and one of the daughters served in Africa as a member of a missionary community. Mary again began thinking that God was calling her to become a religious. In a home not far from where Mary was living, Holy Cross sisters from the hospital in nearby Ingsbohl were caring for a sick man. She described her encounter with them: *They were there in the family as private nurses. One time, one of them asked me to stay with her for a night, as she feared to be alone with the sick man. I did so, and learned to love to wait on the sick. A short time after, I entered that Convent. . . .*

Go to America!

As a postulant, Mary was assigned to the hospital. Although she liked the work very much, she continued to feel that God was calling her to something else. Soon another call from God precipitated a major change in her life: *While I was busy at work, I again heard God's voice loud and strong, saying, "Go to America!" At once the thought took possession of me: "Then I'll go to Cincinnati, Ohio." I had seen those two names in the newspaper, and they had attracted me . . . .*

One can imagine the commotion she caused when she shared this message with others. She did not say how she informed the sisters that God was telling her to leave their postulancy and go to America. When she arrived at home, she told her brother of her decision. Even though Mary was in her late 20s, had her own money, and had lived independently, custom required that, since she was living under her brother's roof, he would have to give his permission for her to go to America. He refused to take her seriously, but told her she could join any one of the 12 communities in the neighborhood. Mary described her reaction to his refusal:

My mind, however, was settled and determined about going to America. I went repeatedly to the Bureau of Information, but no one cared to . . . help me. I even went to St. Gall to find about permits and tickets and the cost, but could get no satisfaction. Then I turned to my Heavenly Mother and made a pilgrimage to Our Lady of Perpetual Help.

I made an agreement with the Queen of Heaven to help me obtain everything necessary for the voyage on her feast of the Visitation [July 2], otherwise, I would give up trying to get to America.

Mary's simple faith and reliance on heavenly help brought results. On July 2, 1882, when she was 30 years old, things came together for her. She wrote: *On the feast at 10:00 a.m. . . , everything had changed. My brother gave his permission, the pastor was satisfied, the man at the bureau got busy, and when evening came, all arrangements had been made.*

Eagerly, Mary awaited the day of her departure. At last it was time to board the train taking her to the seaport where she would begin her voyage. Apparently the crossing was uneventful, since she did not comment on it. After she arrived in America, she made her way to Cincinnati, the city she had heard about while in Europe. She had no other plans except to follow the will of God, who she firmly believed was directing her.

Cincinnati, Ohio

In Cincinnati, Mary sought accommodations with the Franciscan Sisters of the Poor. The sisters, hearing of Mary's experience in hospital work, no doubt realized they could help her while she helped them in their work. They were, at that time, building St. Elizabeth Hospital, near downtown Dayton, Ohio, and they suggested that Mary go there to work. She worked at the hospital for a few months, being there for its dedication in 1882. She enjoyed nursing the sick, but her mind was still restless. Again she waited for a sign or message from God. She trusted that God, who had led her this far, would continue to guide her. She wrote:

It was Christmas now, and some Sisters of the Precious Blood were in Dayton buying things. They came to the hospital. One of the sisters was Sister Nathalia Josberger. I met her in the kitchen. While I was watching her with some curiosity, loud and clear came the voice of God, "To that Order you belong!" This time it pierced me through and through.

Sisters of the Precious Blood

When Mary told the Franciscan sisters she was leaving their employment because she heard God calling her to join the Sisters of the Precious Blood, once again she was met with undisguised skepticism. The sisters had found Mary to be a good worker and an asset to their nursing staff. They asked her to wait for a while and remain with them as she prayed for guidance in this decision. But Mary reacted as she had in Europe when she heard the voice of God telling her to go to Rome. She was determined to find a way to respond to this new call. Describing her urgency, she wrote:

> *. . . I had no rest and on St. Stephen's Day [Dec. 26] I reached Maria Stein [convent]. Here I was made to wait quite a long time in the waiting room. I felt quite strange and lonely so I made up my mind to simply slip out of the door and find my way somehow to the [Franciscan] Sisters in Dayton, when the Mysterious Voice spoke determinedly and clearly. "No, you may not leave; right here you stay."*
>
> *Very much scared, but obedient, I sat down again. Then the door opened and in came Mother Kunigunda and Sister Appia [Scherrieb]. They took me along into the refectory where the Sisters were eating dinner. They were all eating so heartily, that I sat down and followed suit, eating with a good appetite, and strange to say—I felt at home.*

Mary brought with her to Maria Stein knowledge of five languages, as well as valuable experience from her travels in

130

Europe. Educated, independent and self-directed, she had cared for children of wealthy parents and had experience nursing the sick. All this she humbly placed before the Congregation to use as needed. The Congregational Archives say simply that "Mary Gschwend entered the Community on December 26, 1882 at Maria Stein, Ohio at age 30."

Life in the Community

Convents of the Sisters of the Precious Blood at that time were self-sustaining. Sisters living in each one were expected to do all the work necessary to support the local community. Young women desiring to enter were absorbed into the Community with no formal postulancy or novitiate. The local superior was responsible for their spiritual formation and integration into community life.

Although Mary was accepted into the Congregation at Maria Stein, records show that very soon she was sent to join the local community at Thompson, Ohio. There she was assigned to cut wood for the fireplaces, to cook, and to work in the fields. She also assisted in the task of greeting pilgrims who came to the Shrine of the Sorrowful Mother. This Shrine had been built by Father Francis de Sales Brunner in 1850 and enlarged in 1870.

Mary, who received the name of Sister Mary Ildephonsa at some point early in her religious life, humbly accepted the assignments given to her. She wrote of these early days:

> I have never felt in the least dissatisfied, even though I was called upon to do field work, to which I was absolutely unaccustomed and which was quite hard for me, but the assurance never left me that I was at the place where my Heavenly Father wished me to be.

The record of Ildephonsa's 60 years of ministry in the Community is rather vague and incomplete. It lists simply "domestic work," along with the places she served, without dates. At some point, she had a mishap at work which she described as *an injury, from which I shall suffer as long as I live*. A

131

deformity of her back, quite noticeable in her later years, may have been evidence of this misfortune.

In 1889, seven years after her arrival at Maria Stein, Mary became a novice at St. Mary's Home, Indiana. One year later she professed her vows. Prior to 1887 when separate CPPS communities for men and women came into being, members took an Oath of Allegiance to the Society rather than vows. The fact that Ildephonsa did not make a novitiate—a formal study program initiating young women into religious life— when she first entered, or make vows for many years was not unusual. It was the custom of the times. Women entering the Congregation simply began to live in a convent learning how to be a religious through the guidance of the local superior and the example of the other sisters.

Ildephonsa grew in holiness as she aged. Her life, seemingly humdrum and marked by servitude, was a life lived for God alone. The special favors given to her in her early life may or may not have continued through all those years of work. In 1929 after 47 years of service and at age 77, she was permitted to retire from active service at Salem Heights Motherhouse in Dayton.

Her assigned occupation was to "Pray, eat and sleep." For the next 13 years, she was free to spend most of her days and nights in prayer nourishing her special relationship with God.

Sister Ildephonsa Gschwend

Stories of Ildephonsa

Sisters who knew Ildephonsa still tell stories about her closeness to God. During the day, novices, as official worshipers, were assigned to pray for an hour on two prie-dieus near the communion rail in the motherhouse chapel. Ildephonsa would often kneel between them on the floor or in the first pew waiting for the novices to leave so she could replace them. She wanted to be as close as possible to the exposed Blessed Sacrament where, some sisters say, she saw the face of Jesus. Often, as she knelt there, she could be heard saying *You have such pretty eyes.*

As long as she was able, Ildephonsa spent most of her waking hours in chapel, sometimes exhibiting a sense of proprietorship about what happened there. Sister Leonidas Piekenbrock, a novice at the time, recalls that Ildephonsa would pull the habits of the kneeling novices over their shoes to make it look nicer. On dark and dreary days, she would bring a small vigil light to the prie-dieu so the novices could see better.

Sister Florentine Gregory remembers that Ildephonsa liked to pray on the prie-dieus. Though she would be almost falling over in sleep, she refused to give up her closeness to the Blessed Sacrament. Day and night, the frail, bent-over nun would be seen praying for hours on end.

One day Sister Leandra Droll was dusting the main altar at Salem Heights with the Blessed Sacrament exposed. Mother Magna Lehman saw Leandra on the altar and called her to come down, scolding, "You should not be dusting on the altar during exposition." Of course, since the Blessed Sacrament was exposed 24 hours a day, there was no other time to dust. After Mother Magna left, Ildephonsa approached Leandra and said, *Do not be disturbed by Mother's words, Jesus looked over to you and smiled.* Idelphonsa often spoke of seeing *her prince* in human form.

Idelphonsa ended her autobiography with these words:

I served God now for fifty-six years in religion, having entered the convent December 26, 1882. I feel age coming on, sight and hearing are no longer keen, and I get tired even without exertion of any kind. The Superiors are very considerate, and the old Sisters can rest whenever they need it.

I am sorry now that I did not persevere in trying to do needle-work when I was young—I might have been able to make myself useful in old age. I pray instead, and remain often for hours in the Chapel near the Tabernacle or Altar. Now I am tired—also of writing. Hope the Sisters pray for me, that I may always be able to practice patience.

Ildephonsa completed her story in 1938. She died on May 3, 1942 after two months of a flu-related illness. Her obituary briefly outlines when she entered, where she ministered, and when she died. Her autobiography and the stories about her by the sisters reveal a bit more. The Sisters of the Precious Blood treasure the memory of a woman who lived a life of humble service, and whom God favored in a special way.

Chapel of the Immaculate Conception at Salem Heights
where Ildephonsa spent most of her time after she retired.

Sources

As in previous volumes of this series, much of the material was taken from the Archives of the Congregation. The Internet provided general geographical and historical information.

Primary sources for Congregational history include:

Chronicles of the Sisters of the Precious Blood. Unpublished.

CPPS Heritage Series, Volume I "The Work of Their Hands," by Cordelia Gast. Publications, Graphics & Designs, Denver, CO, 2002.

CPPS Legacy Series, The Legacy Continues. . . , Volumes I, II, & III. *WovenWord Press, Boulder, CO, 2000, 2001, & 2002.*

Gutman, Sister Mildred CPPS. *Not With Silver or Gold.* St. Anthony Guild Press, Patterson, NJ, 1945.

Knapke Paul J. CPPS. *American Province CPPS Volume II: Early Years in America 1844-1859.* Messenger Press, Carthagena, OH, 1968.

Richardson, Sister Janet Davis CSJP & Werner, Sister Canice CPPS. *More Than the Doing.* Messenger Press, Carthagena, Ohio, 1995.

Waltz, Sister Mary Adelaide CPPS. *The Voice of Praise.* Unpublished History of the Sisters of the Precious Blood, 1936.

Illustrations

All photos were taken from the Archives of the Sisters of the Precious Blood, except the ones on pp 123, 124 and 126 which are in the public domain.

To obtain copies of this book or
Volumes I, II or III of the
Legacy Series, or
Volume I of the
Heritage Series,
contact:

Sisters of the Precious Blood
4000 Denlinger Road
Dayton, OH   45426

(937) 837-3302
Srs.CPPS@spbdo.com